The New Students' Companion

The New Students' Companion

A treasure house of knowledge

Meenakshi

BLUEJAY

Bluejay Books Pvt. Ltd.
A-8/76, 1st Floor Sector 16,
Rohini Delhi 110085
info@bluejaybooksindia.com

First published in 2014 by
Bluejay Books Pvt. Ltd.

Typeset by Eshu Graphic

Printed and bound in India

CONTENTS

1

HISTORY OF INDIA

ANCIENT INDIA : EARLY CIVILISATION

Palaeolithic Age

- The earliest inhabitants of India were called palaeolithic people, because they used stone in making their tools and weapons.
- These people were in the lowest stage of civilisation, ignorant of the use of metal; pottery and art to be found to the south of Narmada in Andhra Pradesh.

Neolithic Age

- The palaeolithic men were followed by neolithic men or men of the new stone age.
- These men were ignorant of the use of metals, except copper; far more civilised than their palaeolithic forerunners.
- They cultivated land, used pottery, and buried the dead bodies.
- Traces of these men have been discovered in most of the states throughout India.
- They domesticated animals like cattle and dogs.

Metal Age

- The Stone Age in India, as in other countries, was followed by what may be called the Metal age, i.e., the age when the use of metals superseded stones in making tools and other implements.
- In northern India, the metal first used was copper and after that, iron.
- In southern India, the use of stone was immediately followed by that of iron, though it was introduced much later than in the north.

Chalcolithic Age: Men used both stone and copper tools.

THE INDUS VALLEY CIVILISATION
(Proto-Historic Inhabitants)

- The excavations at Mohenjodaro (Sind), Harappa (West Punjab), Ropar (East Punjab), Kalibangan (Rajasthan) and Lothal (Gujarat) have testified that an advanced urban civilisation flourished in India between 2500-1750 BC.

Political Life

- The Historians feel that there was a centralised government.
- The weapons of war like axes, spears, daggers, bows and arrows and slings were made of stone.

Social Life

- *Food:* The people of Indus Valley used wheat, rice, barley, milk, dates, fish, eggs and animal flesh.
- *Dress:* They used both cotton and woollen clothes.
- *Ornaments:* They were made of gold, silver, ivory, copper and precious stones for the rich. For the poor,

these were made of shell of terracotta used by men and women.

- *Amusements:* The Indus Valley people amused themselves by hunting, fishing, rearing animals, birds, reading, and writing.

Economic Life

- These people were *good traders* whose transport on land was the bullock cart, while boats were used in the rivers and sea.
- These people were dependent upon agriculture as they grew wheat, barley, rice, dates and cotton.
- Animal rearing was another source of income as they domesticated cattle, camels, elephants, pigs, fowls and dogs. *Iron* was not known. They established commercial contacts with the Sumerians.

Art and Architecture

- *Great builders:* Their drainage system was par excellence. They built planned cities.
- *Crafts:* Potters used to paint pottery, children's toys like rattles and whistles. Other crafts included spinning and weaving of cotton and wool. The granary at Harappa was made of bricks.

Religious Life

- The Indus Valley people worshipped Mother Goddess, Siva, stones, trees (especially *pipal* tree) and animals (especially *bulls* and *snakes).*
- The male God worshipped by them was *Pasupati.*

Decline

The main causes of the decline of Indus Valley Civilisation were:

- Destruction due to Aryan invasion;
- Recurring floods;
- Decreasing fertility of soil due to overexploitation;
- Deforestation leading to extension of deserts; and
- Occasional earthquakes.

However, this civilisation did not come to a sudden end; it faded away gradually.

THE VEDIC AGE : THE ARYANS

Coming of the Aryans into India

- The European scholars place the period of their coming between 2000 BC and 1500 BC. They occupied North India, pushing the Dravidians to the South.

Political Life

- In the early Vedic age, the Aryans used to live in villages or *grams.*
- The head of a village was called *Gramani.*
- The affairs of a village were managed by an elected *Panchayat.*
- Every tribe or *jana* had one chief who was called *Rajan.* He was mostly hereditary, but was sometimes elected.
- The chief duty of the king was the protection of the territory and welfare of his subjects.
- The *Rajan* was helped by several officers like the Royal Priest *(Purohit),* Commander-in-Chief *(Senani)* and the Head of the village *(Gramani).*
- The priest was a distinguished officer. He was a sort of Chief Minister.

- The king had two elected assemblies, called the *Samiti* and the *Sabha*. These bodies exercised a check on the absolute power of the king.

Social Life

- Their culture was *pastoral.*
- Aryans had a joint family system. The father was known as *Grihapati.*
- In Vedic society, women were held in great respect. There was no *purdah.* Their education pertained to language, literature, fine arts like dancing and music and military science. Child marriage and *Sati* system were not known.
- Food and clothing of the Aryans were very simple.
- There was no rigid caste system among the early Aryans.
- Education stressed on character building.
- The Aryans were fond of dancing, wrestling, boxing, diving, listening to the bards and chariot-racing.

Economic Life

- The main occupation of the Aryans was agriculture. They used to plough the land and grow crops.
- Cattle-rearing was another occupation. Cow was considered very sacred.
- They were very good at weaving cloth, tanning leather and making ornaments. There were carpenters, blacksmiths, goldsmiths, tanners, potters and weavers.
- The barter system was popular in trade.

Religious Life

- The Aryans were lovers of nature. They were influenced by the powers of nature, e.g., the sun, water and fire.
- In the Aryan period, there was no idol worship.
- *Yajna* or *havan* was an essential part of the Aryan religion.
- The Aryans were the originators of the Hindu civilisation.

Religious Books

- The *Vedas* are the most sacred books of the Hindus. They are four in number : *Rig Veda,* in the praise of God; *Yajur Veda* contains *mantras* for the performance of Yajnas; *Sam Veda* contains musical chants; while *Atharva Vada* contains magical chants. *Rig Veda* is the oldest Veda.
- The *Upanishads* deal with Aryan philosophy and theology. They elaborate the main problems of man, viz., "What is God? What is Soul? What is Matter? How are they related?"
- *Manu Smriti:* Manu was the great lawgiver of the Aryan period. His book *Manu Smriti* deals with laws of inheritance, duties of kings, four *varnas* and the four *ashramas.*
- The *Puranas* are eighteen in number, the most important being the *Bhagawata Purana* and the *Vishnu Purana.* The former describes the life story of Lord Krishna while the latter deals with Lord Vishnu and his various incarnations.
- The *Brahamanas:* These books deal with ritualism.

THE LATER VEDIC PERIOD

- The Aryans settled in the valleys of the Ganga and the Yamuna.
- Two important epics-the Ramayana and the Mahabharata – reflect the social, religious, economic and political conditions of India in the later Vedic period.
- The original name of *Mahabharata* was *'Jaya Samhita'*.

Political Conditions

- The political conditions of the Aryans were more developed than those in the early Vedic period. The tiny tribal settlements of the Vedic period were replaced by strong kingdoms.
- The *Ramayana* and the *Mahabharata* mention such kingdoms, e.g., Kurus, Panchalas, Koshala (Oudh), Videha (North Bihar), Kashi, Matsya, etc. These were small republics, but there were no big empires.
- The power of the kings increased immensely and kingship became hereditary. Instead of *Rajan,* they came to be called *Samrat.* As a result, the importance of the *Sabha* and the *Samiti* declined.
- The chief source of government income was land revenue, which was *one-sixth* of the produce.
- A regular army was maintained. It consisted of four arms: Cavalry, Infantry, Chariots and Elephants.

Economic Conditions

- Agriculture, cattle-rearing, trade and industry had made great progress.
- Many crafts were practised. The merchants were organised.

Social Conditions

- There was a growth of big cities like Ayodhya, Indraprastha and Mathura. The caste system became more defined and rigid.
- People were mostly vegetarian. The rich men were addicted to gambling and drinking.
- Women enjoyed the same freedom as men and received Vedic education. But the status of women was much higher in the Rig Vedic period. It deteriorated progressively and women came to depend more and more on their husbands.
- Education was free and universal. There were several *ashramas* in the forests where *Brahmins* lived with their students and taught them.

Religious Conditions

- The Vedic religion had undergone a great change. In the Epic or later Vedic period; religion became very close to modern Hinduism.
- It came to be called Brahmanical Hinduism.

Caste System

- The Hindu society was divided into various groups or families. Such a group was called caste.
- In the beginning, this division was based on occupation. Later, the caste system became hereditary and rigid.
- The Aryans were split up into four groups according to occupations-(*i*) *Brahmins* or the priestly class; *(ii) Kshatriyas* or the military class; *(iii) Vaishyas* or the trading class, farmers and artisans; *(iv) Shudras* or the labour class.

Growth of Jainism and Buddhism

The period around 6th century BC was marked by religious unrest. The reasons were:

- Vedic rites had become very elaborate and costly.
- Dominance of priestly class or Brahmins who had become unscrupulous and dishonest.
- Difficult and outdated language used for religious ceremonies, beyond common man's understanding. Buddhism and Jainism grew out of this unrest.

Vardhamana Mahavira

- He was born in 599 BC.
- He was the founder of Jainism.
- He was the 24th Tirthankar (Path Finder) of the Jains.
- He was the son of a Vaishali noble.
- He joined the order of Parshvanath (the 23rd Tirthankar) and attained supreme knowledge.
- He was a great exponent of Jainism. He died in 468 BC at Pawapuri (Nalanda district), now in Bihar.

Jainism

- It is a non-Brahmanical system. Its founder was Mahavira.
- The chief doctrines of Jainism are *Tri Ratna* or *Three -Jewels,* i.e., every Jain must believe in three things: Right faith; Right knowledge; Right conduct.
- They believe in the doctrine of non-violence.
- They are silent about the existence of God.
- According to them, the highest aim of life is *Nirvana.*

- Jainism is divided into two sects: *Svetambara* (white-clad) and *Digambara* (sky-clad)
- Their sacred books are *Angas* and *Purvas.*

Gautam Buddha

- He was born in 563 BC at Lumbini (now in Nepal).
- He was the son of Suddodhana, a prince of Sakya clan ruling Kapilavastu.
- He attained enlightenment at Bodh Gaya and delivered his first sermon at Sarnath.
- He died at Kushinagar.

Buddhism

- It rose against the background of Hinduism in North India in the 6th century BC.
- Its founder was Gautama Siddhartha, popularly known as Buddha.
- Its main sacred books are *Tripitakas.* The main precepts of Buddhism are:
    - *The Four Great Truths,* viz., *(a)* the world is full of misery; *(b)* the cause of pain and misery is desire or craving; *(c)* the pain can be ended by killing or controlling the desires; *(d)* the desires can be controlled by the Eight-Fold path.
    - *The Eight-Fold Path:* It consists of Right Belief, Right Thought, Right Action, Watchfulness, Right Speech and Right Meditation.
    - *Belief in Nirvana:* The more one acquires merit by following the eight-fold path, the sooner the *Nirvana* or freedom from the cycle of birth and death is obtained.

- *Belief in Ahimsa:* One should not cause injury to any living being—animal or man.
- *Law of Karma:* The man reaps the fruit of his deeds done in the past. If anyone does noble deeds in this world, he will get his reward in the next birth. *Jatakas* are the Buddhist religious books.

Buddhist Councils

- *The First Council* was held at Rajagriha in 483 BC, soon after the death of Buddha, under the auspices of Ajatshatru.
- Buddha's disciples Upali and Ananda recited the *Vinaya Pitaka* or the rules of order and *Sutta Pitaka,* respectively. The latter contained Buddha's sermons.
- It was presided over by Mahakassapa.
- *The Second Council* was held at Vaishali about 383 BC, under the auspices of King Kalasoka or Kakavarnin.
- It led to the first division of Buddhism into *Stharvadins* and *Mahasanghikas.* It was presided over by Sabakami.
- *The Third Council* was convened by Ashoka at Patliputra in 250 BC.
- It added some Pali scriptures dealing with psychology and metaphysics. It was presided over by Tisa Mongaliputta.
- *The Fourth Council* was convened by Kanishka in 72 AD near Kundalavana (Kashmir). It was presided over by Vasumitra.
- It formally recognised the division of Budhism into the great and lesser vehicles, *Mahayana* and *Hinayana,* respectively.

The Magadha Empire

- From 6th century BC to 4th century BC, the political scene in India is vague from the historical point of view.
- Magadha was the most powerful kingdom in North India. Its capital was Pataliputra. Notable rulers were *Bimbisara* (founder) and *Ajatshatru.*
- They were followed by weak successors till the foundation of the *Nanda dynasty.* The tyranny of the Nanda rulers could not win popularity. They were finally overthrown by Chandragupta Maurya.
- The greatest contribution of the Nandas was their effort to give political unity to the country.

Alexander's Invasion (327-326 BC)

- At the time of invasion of India by Alexander, India was ruled by petty kings in the north-west region.
- Alexander defeated Porus, the king of the territory between Jhelum and Chenab rivers.
- The invasion had lasting effect on India – political unification by the petty kings, cultural exchange and writing the contemporary history of India by Greek historians, etc.
- Alexander died at Babylon.

MAURYA DYNASTY (321-185 BC)

Chandragupta Maurya (321-298 BC)

- He was the founder of the Maurya dynasty.
- He defeated Seleucus, the General of Alexander, in 305 BC.
- He founded an excellent system of municipal administration and military organisation.

Megasthenese

- He was the ambassador of Seleucus in the court of Chandragupta Maurya.
- He lived in Pataliputra for five years from 302 BC.
- His account of India is given in *Indica,* which exists today only in parts and throws light on the political and social conditions of that age.

Kautilya (Chanakya)

- He was the Chief Minister of Chandragupta Maurya and an authority on Political Science in the 4th century BC.
- He wrote *Arthashastra,* which can be roughly translated as a treatise on 'Statehood'.

Bindusara (298-273 BC)

- He was the son of Chandragupta Maurya.
- His empire extended throughout the whole of northern India and parts of Deccan.

Ashoka (273-232 BC)

- He was one of the best and the ablest rulers in world history.
- He embraced Buddhism after the bloody war of Kalinga (261 BC), for he was greatly moved by the loss of human lives in this war. The rest of his life was devoted towards the propagation of Buddhism.
- His inscriptions on rocks and pillars (in Prakrit language) are a source of great historical knowledge.
- Ashoka was converted into Buddhism by Upagupta. He built a stupa at Sanchi. His name is inscribed on Maski edict.

The Sunga Dynasty (185-151 BC)

- About 185 BC., *Pushyamitra,* who was the Commander-in-Chief of the last Maurya King Brihadratha, killed his master and became the founder of the Sunga dynasty of Magadha.
- He was an orthodox Hindu who started the revival of the Brahmanical Movement.
- They also built *Garuda Pillar* at Besnagar.

Kanva Dynasty (75-30 BC)

- Vasudeva Kanva, who was the minister of the last Sunga King, killed his master and occupied the throne around 75 BC.
- The Kanva dynasty was the dynasty of four kings who ruled for about 45 years.

Satavahana Dynasty (235-30 BC)

- Sometimes called the Andhras, this dynasty was established in the 3rd century BC by *Simukha.*
- It lasted for about 450 years.
- Its main areas were the Deccan and Western India with *Pratisthana* as its capital.
- They built *Chaitya temples* in Karle and Amravati stupa.
- They were the first to give grants for religious beneficiaries.

Kharavela, Sakas, Satraps and Parthians (40-78 AD)

- Kalinga reached the zenith of its glory under the *Kalingraj* (Kharvel), but his empire vanished soon after.

- This Jain kingdom threw off the yoke of the Mauryas some time after the death of Ashoka.
- These were foreigners of Central Asia, who came to India in search of conquest and settled in India.

KUSHAN DYNASTY (40-162 AD)

Kanishka (78-120 AD)

- He was the greatest of Kushan rulers in India.
- His territories extended up to Yarkand. His capital was Pashawar (Purushapura).
- Like Ashoka, he was a great patron of Buddhism and convened the *Fourth Buddhist Council* at Srinagar.
- In his days, Buddhism was divided into two sects, *Hinayana* (lesser vehicle) and *Mahayana* (greater vehicle).
- The *Hinayana* comprised followers of old religion. They looked upon Buddha simply as a *guru* or Great Master and were opposed to idol worship.
- The *Mahayanis* raised Buddha to the position of a saviour god and worshipped the idols of Buddha with great rituals.
- Gandhara School of Art (Graeco-Buddhist style) rose to its zenith during his reign.
- It specialised in the images of Buddha in sitting form with a 'Chakra' in the back and shows great Greek influence.
- *The Saka Era* begins from the date of his accession.
- Gold coins were issued for the first time by Kushana.

Asvaghosha

- He was a many-sided genius, who adorned the court of Kanishka.
- He was the author of *Buddhacharita.*
- The great exponents of the Mahayana, Vasumitra, Nagarjuna and Charak (great physician) also adorned his court.

Mathura School of Sculpture

- It was purely indigenous and not exotic. Red stone was used extensively.
- It was influenced by Gandhara School of art.

GUPTA DYNASTY (320-550 AD)

- Sri Gupta was the founder of the Gupta dynasty.
- The Gupta period is known as the Golden Period of Hinduism in India.
- The Guptas freed the country from foreign domination.
- Art, science and literature were cultivated with success and distinction.
- Ajanta Caves were built between 300 and 700 AD during the Gupta period. Most of them professed faith in Brahminism.
- They built the Iron Pillar at Mehrauli in Delhi.
- The temples at Bhitargaon and Deogarh are special examples of Gupta architecture.

Chandragupta I (320-335 AD)

- He was the first great ruler of the Mauryan Dynasty.
- Gupta rule started from 320 AD during his reign.

Samudragupta (335-375 AD)

- He was a great scholar, poet and musician.
- He is known as the *Indian Napoleon* on account of his conquests.
- He was a worshipper of Vishnu but tolerant of Buddhism also.
- He erected the Allahabad Pillar, the inscription on which was composed by Harisena.

Chandragupta II (375-413 AD)

- He is generally identified with the legendary Vikramaditya.
- During his reign, the Gupta empire was at the height of its power.
- He was a liberal patron of arts and literature.
- The Chinese pilgrim Fa-Hien visited India during his time. He says that the country was rich and the people led a moral and honest life. Taxes were very light and kingdoms and its people were secure.

Kumaragupta I (413-455 AD)

- He was the son of Chandragupta II.
- Towards the end of his reign, he was attacked by Pushyamitra (from the west) and the Huns. With him ended the golden era of the Guptas.

Skandagupta (455-477 AD)

- He was the last great ruler of this dynasty.
- His reign was short and stormy as the Huns made their fierce raids in his time.

The Huns

- The Huns were a wild and fierce nomadic tribe of Europe.
- In the middle of the 5th century AD, they were repulsed by Skandagupta, the grandson of Chandragupta Vikramaditya, the then ruler.
- At the end of the 5th century AD, they made a more determined attack and their chief, *Tormana,* captured Punjab, Rajputana, Sind and Malwa after overthrowing the Gupta ruler there.
- Eventually, Huns were absorbed into the Rajput population.

PUSHYABHUTI DYNASTY (560-647 AD)

Harshavardhana (606-647 AD)

- His capital was Kannauj.
- He was the author of *Nagananda* and *Ratnavali.*
- *Banabhatta,* the famous poet lived during his reign.
- He is considered to be the last great Hindu king of North India.
- He was a staunch follower of Buddhism.
- He was also a follower of the Sun God.

Hiuen Tsang

- Hiuen tsang was a Chinese pilgrim, who visited India during the reign of King Harshavardhana.
- He stayed in India from 629 to 645 AD and visited Buddhist pilgrimage centres.
- He has left interesting accounts of the conditions of India at that time.

- According to him, Nalanda University was at its peak during his visit.

The Rajputs (650-1200 AD)

- The Rajputs dominated the Indian political scene for about 500 years.

The well-known Rajput rulers were:

- Prithviraj Chauhan, who ruled over Delhi and Ajmer and defeated Mohammad Ghori in 1191 in the *First Battle of Tarain.* He was defeated and killed by Ghori in 1192 in the *Second Battle of Tarain.*
- Jai Chand Rathaur, the last famous Rajput king, was also defeated and killed by Mohammad Ghori in 1194.
- The *Palas* who ruled in Bihar and the *Senas* who ruled in Bengal.
- The *Parmars,* the most famous of whom was King Bhoja, ruled in Malwa.
- The *Chandels* ruled in Bundelkhand till Qutab-ud-din Aibak conquered it in 1203.
- Chittor was the most important Rajput kingdom.
- Rana Kumbha was a famous ruler of this dynasty. He defeated Mahmud Khilji and erected a Victory Tower in Chittor.
- His son Rana Sangram Singh (Sanga) and Rana Pratap were other great rulers of this kingdom.

Salient Features of Rajput Rule

- The country remained free of invasions but lost foreign contacts and became insular. The national character degenerated.

Social Life:

- The caste system was rigid. The Rajputs were proud and warlike but hospitable. The social vices such as Sati, child marriage and female infanticide were also prevalent.
- Culturally, many great fortresses and temples were built, such as the temples at Khajuraho (Madhya Pradesh) and Bhubaneswar (Orissa), the Sun Temple at Konark, Jagannath Temple at Puri, and Dilwara Jain Temples at Mount Abu.
- Jayadeva was a great poet of the period. He wrote the *Gita Govinda.*
- He lived at the court of Laxman Sen of Bengal.
- The downfall of the Rajputs is attributed to lack of unity and foresightedness, rigid caste system, geographical impediments, defective military organisation and absence of a national leader. Greed and fanaticism of the Muslim invaders also was a major cause.

Sangam Age

- In this age, successive assemblies of Tamil poets were held at Madurai and several anthologies of Tamil poems were compiled.
- The age refers to the history of South India between 300 BC and 300 AD.

Pallavas of Kanchi

- After the fall of the Andhras in the third century AD, the Pallavas came into prominence.
- Their first great king was Sivaskanda Varman.

- The Pallavas were patrons of Sanskrit and Brahminism.
- They were very prominent from the middle of the 6th century to the middle of the 8th century.
- They were constantly at war with the Chalukyas in the North and the Cholas in the South.
- The dynasty of great Pallavas was founded by the Simahavishnu, father of Mahendra Varman I.
- The Pallavas are remembered for temple architecture, especially rock-cut *raths* (Seven Pagodas) at Mahabalipuram.
- Their capital was Kanchipuram.

Mahendra Varman I (600-625 AD)

- He was one of the greatest Pallava kings.
- He was defeated by Pulakesin II.
- He was converted to Saivism from Jainism.
- He is remembered for his contribution to the rock-cut temples.

Narasimha Varman (625-645 AD)

- He was the most famous and powerful of the Pallava kings.
- He defeated and killed Pulakesin II and sent a naval expedition to Sri Lanka.
- He founded the city, Mamallapuram, the modern day Mahabalipuram.

Chalukyas of Vatapi (Badami)

- The Chalukyas came to power in the 6th century in Karnataka with their capital at Vatapi in the Bijapur district.

- The founder of this dynasty was Pulkesin I. Aihole is the site well-known for Chalukyan architecture.

Pulakesin II (609-642 AD)

- He was the most famous ruler. His greatest achievement was his victory over Harshavardhan in 620 AD.
- He defeated the Pallava king Mahendra Varman I and established an empire extending from the Narmada to the Cauvery.
- He was killed by Pallava ruler Narasimha Varman, who stormed Vatapi in 642 AD.

Rashtrakutas (733-973 AD)

- In 733, Dantidurga overthrew the Chalukya power and founded the kingdom of Rashtrakutas of Karnataka and Maharashtra.
- This kingdom extended from south Gujarat, Malwa and Bundelkhand in the north to Tanjore in the south. They were considered to be the greatest rulers of the time.
- They had their capital at *Malkhed,* near Sholapur.
- During the reign of Krishna I, the rock-cut temple of Kailasha at Ellora was carved. Dhruva, another able king, defeated Dharmapala of Bengal and Mihira Bhoja, the Pratihara King.
- Govinda III was the most powerful king of the Rashtrakutas.
- During the reign of Krishna II, Kailash Temple at Ellora was built.
- The *Elephanta caves* were also built during this period.

Chalukyas of Kalyani

- The new dynasty of Chalukyas was founded by

Tailapa II in 973 AD by overthrowing the Rashtrakutas.

- Their capital was Kalyani (Gujarat). They ruled up to the 12th century.

Hoysalas of Dwarsamudra

- This dynasty ruled the Mysore region at the beginning of the 12th century in subordination to the Chalukyas but helped a lot in the revival of Hinduism (Vaishnavism).
- The dynasty ended with the sacking of Dwarsamudra by Malik Kafur, the general of Ala-ud-din Khilji.
- Many temples were built by them, including the Halebid temples in Karnataka.
- Their capital was Dwarsamudra.

Pandya Dynasty

- The Pandyas were subjects of the Pallavas of Kanchi.
- Their capital was Madurai.
- In the 11th and 12th centuries, they were tributary to the Cholas, but later became the chief Tamil power in the South.
- Their kingdom declined after the Muslim invasion in 1310.

Chera Dynasty

- This was another Tamil kingdom.
- Senguttuvan, the *Talchera* was the famous King of Chera Dynasty.
- Their kingdom included greater part of Travancore and they were subsidiary to the powerful Cholas.

Chola Dynasty

- It was also an ancient Tamil kingdom ruling over Tamil Nadu and parts of Karnataka.
- It was founded by Vijayalaya in 850 AD, who defeated Pandyas of the south and occupied their capital Madurai.
- The Chola empire is known for local self-government of village autonomy.
- It was under Cholas that *overseas conquests* were undertaken because of their *naval power.*
- The Cholas occupied Pegu in Burma (Myanmar), Sumatra, Malaya and the Andaman and Nicobar Islands.
- Their capital was *Tanjore.*
- *Vimana style of architecture* reached its zenith during their reign.

Rajaraja Chola (985-1014 AD)

- He established the supremacy of the Chola power in the south.
- He built the *Brihadeswara Temple* at Tanjore (Thanjavur).

Rajendra Chola (1014-1044 AD)

- He extended the dominions of the Chola kingdom.
- His fleet crossed the Bay of Bengal with an army and conquered a number of states in Sumatra, Java and Malaya.
- He built a new capital, Gangaikonda-cholapuram to commemorate his victory in the north.

OTHER KINGS

Lalitaditya (733-769 AD)

- He was the most renowned of the kings of Kashmir.
- He defeated Yasovarman, the King of Kannauj, in 740 AD.
- He built the famous *Martanda Temple* dedicated to the Sun God.

Yasovarman of Kannauj

- He was a vigorous ruler in Kannauj after Harsha in the 8th century.
- He was the patron of the great dramatist, *Bhavabhuti.*

Dharmapala (770-810 AD)

- Pala dynasty was founded by Gopala in 750 AD. But the real founder of the great *Pala* dynasty which ruled Bengal was Dharmapala.
- He was defeated by the Rashtrakuta King, Dhruva.
- He was a Buddhist and ruled kannauj for some time.
- He founded the *Vikramashila monastery.*

Devapala (810-850 AD)

- He was the most powerful of the rulers of the Pala dynasty.
- He resisted the invasion of Huns successfully and defeated Mihir Bhoja of Kannauj.
- He raised Bengal to the highest pinnacle of power and prestige.
- After him, the Gauda (Bengal) empire disintegrated.

Mihir Bhoja (836-885 AD)

- He was the greatest *Pratihara (Parihara)* emperor, who ruled from Kannauj.
- He was defeated by Dhruva, the Rashtrakuta king.

MEDIEVAL INDIA

Advent of Turks in India

- Arab traders had been coming to India before Islam was founded.
- Muslims had their relations with South India (Malabar coast in particular) before they came to North India.
- Mohammed-bin-Qasim was the first Arab commander to conquer a portion of India-Sindh in 712 AD.
- He was the son of Subuktigin. He was a great conqueror and warrior of his time. His greatest ambition was to become the master of the whole of Asia and to build an Asian empire. India's immense wealth attracted him and he carried out 17 invasions to the country between 1000 to 1026 AD to plunder the wealth of India with a view to finance his expeditions in Asia.
- His court poet was Firdausi who wrote *Shahnama* in his honour.
- Al-Beruni, the historian, who had accompanied the king to India during his expeditions, has given a reliable description of the invasions and Indian conditions.

GHORI DYNASTY (1186-1206 AD)

Mohammad Ghori (1186-1206 AD)

- In 1186, he occupied Lahore.

- He was defeated by Prithvi Raj, the ruler of Delhi and Ajmer, in the first Battle of Tarain in 1191.
- He defeated Prithvi Raj at Tarain in 1192 in the second battle and laid the foundation of Muslim rule in India.

SLAVE DYNASTY (1206-1290 AD)

Qutubuddin Aibak (1206-1290 AD)

- He was the founder of the Slave dynasty.
- He himself was a slave and the general of Mohammad Ghori.
- After Ghori's death, he became the ruler of his Indian possessions.
- During his reign, he built a mosque (Quwat-ul-Islam) at Delhi and started the famous Qutub Minar, the tallest tower in India.
- It is the first outstanding structure in the Islamic style.

Iltutmish (1210-1236 AD)

- He was the son-in-law of Qutubuddin Aibak.
- He was recognised by the *Khalifa* in 1219 AD.
- Mongols under Genghis Khan attacked India in 1221 AD during his reign.
- He completed the construction of Qutub Minar in 1232, which was begun by Qutubuddin Aibak.

Razia Begum (1236-1239 AD)

- She was the daughter of Iltutmish and the first and only Muslim woman ruler of Delhi.

- She was the most talented and capable child of Iltutmish.
- She was the first ruler among the Sultans of Delhi to take steps to make the powers of the crown absolute.

Nasiruddin Mahmud (1246-1266 AD)

- He was the son of Iltutmish.
- He was very gentle, studious and a pious king.

Ghiasuddin Balban (1266-1287 AD)

- He was a very powerful ruler.
- His greatest achievements are that he saved the empire from Mongol invasion, raised the prestige of the crown and gave the country absolute peace and security.

Kaiqubad (1287-1290 AD)

- He was the last king of the Slave dynasty.
- During his reign Italian traveller *Marco Polo* had visited India on his way to China.
- He was killed by Jalal-ud-din Khilji in 1290 AD.

KHILJI DYNASTY (1290-1320 AD)

Alauddin Khilji (1296-1316 AD)

- He was a great conqueror and reformer.
- Southern India was conquered for the first time by him.
- He shot into fame because of the secularisation of the administration and various civil, military and economic reforms he undertook.

- He enforced a rigid price control system in order to maintain a standing army at small expense.
- He conquered Chittor in 1303 AD.

TUGHLAQ DYNASTY (1320-1412 AD)

Ghiyassuddin Tughlaq (1320-1325 AD)

- He founded the dynasty.
- He built a strong fort named Tughlaqabad near Delhi and strengthened the defences of the northwestern frontier against the danger of recurrent Mongolian attacks.
- He conquered Warangal, put down a revolt in Bengal and made the kingdom's power reach till the southern end of Madurai.

Muhammad-Bin-Tughlaq (1325-1351 AD)

- He was a great scholar and writer, however, some of the novel administrative experiments (such as shifting the capital to Devgiri, new coinage, *etc.),* made him unpopular.
- He is sometimes called the 'Wisest Fool' among the rulers of Delhi.

Firoz Tughlaq (1351-1388 AD)

- He is noted chiefly for works of public utility. He founded new cities, built mosques, hospitals, canals, inns, roads and opened alm houses for the poor and needy.
- He organised Haj pilgrimage at the expense of the state.
- He had founded the Department of Public Works.

SAYYAD DYNASTY (1414-1451 AD)

- This dynasty was established by Khizir Khan, the Viceroy of Timur, in 1414 AD.
- The rule of this dynasty was confined to Delhi and a few surrounding districts.
- The last Sayyad King (Alam Shah) handed over the kingdom to Bahlol Lodhi, the Afghan Governor of Punjab, in 1451 and himself retired.

LODHI DYNASTY (1451-1526 AD)

- Bahlol Lodhi (1451-1489) was the founder of this dynasty.
- The most renowned king of this dynasty was Sikander Lodhi (1489-1517).
- He founded Agra in 1506.
- He was succeeded by Ibrahim Lodhi (1517-1526), who was defeated and killed by Babar at Panipat in 1526.

MUGHAL DYNASTY

Conditions of India before Babar's Invasion

- Politically, there was no powerful kingdom, only several small kingdoms.
- Social evils, malice between Hindus and Muslims persisted in spite of the Bhakti Movement reformers trying to bring about unity.
- Economically, India had abundance of gold and silver. The Hindus were made paupers and the peasants had to face extortion.

Zahiruddin Babar (1526-1530 AD)

- He laid the foundation of the Mughal rule in India. After several unsuccessful invasions of India, he at last defeated Ibrahim Lodhi in the Battle of Panipat in 1526. Thus, the Lodhi rule ended.
- In 1527, Babar defeated Rana Sanga at Kanwah near Fatehpur Sikri.
- In 1529, in the Battle of Gogra, he defeated the Afghans under Mahmud Lodhi. He thus became the master of nearly the whole of northern India.
- Rajputs were defeated because of Babar's generalship, his use of artillery, his scientific tactics and disciplined army, religious zeal of soldiers and the Rajputs, own political errors.
- Babar was a great general, scholar and a literary man.
- But he ignored administration, paid no attention to land revenue, justice, economic matters and public welfare.

Humayun (1530-1540 AD and 1555-1556 AD)

- He could not consolidate the Mughal empire because of political instability, an empty treasury, division of dominions into *jagirs* and family hostility. He also lacked quick decision, sustained efforts, sternness and political insight.
- In 1540, he was defeated by Sher Shah Suri and fled from the country.
- He returned to power only in 1555 after Sher Shah Suri's death.

Suri Dynasty (1540-1555 AD)

- The Suri dynasty is particularly noted for the administration and reforms brought about by Sher Shah Suri (1540-45 AD) in the fields of central and provincial administration, land revenue, police, military and judicial spheres.

- Roads and *sarais* were made to encourage trade; the most important of roads being the Grand Trunk Road.
- Economic conditions improved.
- The currency was reformed, with pure gold and silver coins being struck.
- The postal department was very advanced.
- Education was encouraged through state aid.
- He did not force Hindus to embrace Islam and his attitude towards Hindus was tolerant, though he did destroy some temples.
- Sher Shah, before Akbar, attempted to build an Indian nation by reconciling the followers of divergent racial creeds.
- During his reign, currency notes were first printed.

Akbar (1556-1605 AD)

- He was crowned the emperor of India at the age of 13 at Kalanaur (Punjab).
- He defeated Hemu in the Second Battle of Panipat in 1556 and became the unquestioned master of the country.
- He continued his policy of conquest. He made several conquests, winning against the ruler of Malwa in 1561, against the brave Rani Durgawati of Gondwana in 1564 and so on.
- He captured the fort of Chittor (in Mewar) in 1567.

- Akbar defeated Rana Pratap in the Battle of Haldighati in 1576.

Akbar's Reign – An Assessment

- Akbar's empire extended from Bengal to Afghanistan and Kashmir to Godavari in the South.
- His greatest achievement was the land revenue administration. In times of famine, farmers got loans and the state share was reduced.
- Social reforms included prohibition of child marriage and female infanticide; widow remarriage for Hindus was legalised; forcible conversion to Islam was prohibited, pilgrim tax, *(Jazia)* was abolished, etc.
- Military reforms included Mansabdari system, under which each officer was assigned a rank *(mansab)*. Varying from 10 to 10,000, the *mansab* carried the *Zat* (the personal status and salary) and *Sawar* (the number of cavalry men to be maintained). The system was borrowed from the system followed in Mongolia.
- Religious policy of Akbar is famous for the formulation of *Din-i-Ilahi* in 1582, taking the good points of Hinduism, Islam, Jainism and Sikhism.
- Being a patron of the arts and literature, great scholars like *Abul Fazal,* poets like *Faizi,* statesmen like *Todar Mal,* witty administrators like *Birbal* and musicians like *Tansen* flourished in his court.
- *Tulsidas,* who wrote *Ramcharitmanas,* lived in this period.
- Akbar built Fatehpur Sikri, the forts at Agra, Lahore and Allahabad and Humayun's Tomb at Delhi.

- When he died, he was buried at Sikandra near Agra.
- Akbar is rightly considered the real founder of the Mughal empire in India. Babar could not consolidate the empire and Humayun could not keep it together.

Jahangir(1605-1627 AD)

- He came to the throne on Akbar's death in 1605 AD.
- He is known for his strict administration of justice.
- His wife *Nur Jahan* influenced him a great deal.
- He was a great patron of paintings and *Mansur* was the greatest poet in his court.
- His reforms included striking new coins, abolishing oppressive taxes, construction of more *sarais* for public welfare, freedom of civilians from military oppression, free charitable hospitals, banning slaughter of animals on certain days (in continuation of Akbar's policy), confirmation of land endowments to scholars and religious institutions, prohibition of snatching land from the peasants.
- His reign was marked by several revolts, amidst which Guru Arjan Dev, the fifth Guru of Sikhs, was martyred in 1606 and thus Sikhs were alienated. This was his political blunder.
- His reign first witnessed the coming of European travellers such as Thomas Roe.

Shahjahan (1628-1658 AD)

- His reign is known for promotion of art, culture and architecture.
- The Red Fort, Jama Masjid, Taj Mahal, etc., were built by him.

- In the last years of his life, he was imprisoned by his son, Aurangzeb and died in captivity in 1666.

Aurangzeb (1658-1707 AD)

- He came to the throne after defeating Dara in the Battle of Samugarh in a violent war of succession.
- His reign is marked by ruthless persecution and religious vendetta against the Hindus.
- After his death, the Mughal empire disintegrated.
- His reign was marked by the war with Shivaji, rebellion of Jats, revolt of the Satnamis, martyrdom of Guru Tegh Bahadur, imposition of *Jazia* and war with the Rajputs.
- Aurangzab's failure as a king lay in his fanatical religious policy, his Deccan policy, his suspicious nature and lack of statesmanship.

SALIENT FEATURES OF THE MUGHAL EMPIRE

Administration

- It was a Perso-Arabic system in Indian setting.
- Military type of government.
- Despotic form of government but enlightened, as power was not misused.
- The state was not much concerned with social welfare and reforms.
- Law and justice were not 'modern' and officers were quite corrupt.
- Except for Aurangzeb, the Mughal rule was free of religious intolerance.
- A peculiarity was the manufacture of articles by the state to satisfy its needs.

- The army was formed of infantry, cavalry, artillery, elephantry, navy (mostly used for transport and not war) and supply department.

Economy

- Sources of revenue were land revenue, customs, mint, gifts, confiscations, plunder in wars, salt tax, income from mines and government-controlled factories, pilgrimage tax and *Jazia.*
- Expenditure came under salaries to *mansabdars* and troops, buildings works of public utility, charities, wars and expeditions.
- Agriculture was the chief occupation of the people but there were many famines.
- Industries developed, especially cotton textiles, silk, dyeing, printing, manufacture of wooden and leather articles, weapons, carpets, etc.
- Internal and external trade flourished. Export of textiles, spices, indigo, shawls, etc. and import of gold, silver, raw silk, diamonds, ivory, perfumery, drugs, etc.
- Growth of big and prosperous cities.
- Prices were low but incomes were also low.
- After Aurangzeb, economic conditions deteriorated.

Law and Justice

- The Mughal rulers loved justice. The king's court was supreme.
- Panchayats administered justice in villages.
- The defects were that records of cases were not made, there was corruption and punishments were too harsh.

Society and Religion

- Society was divided on the basis of nobility of status.
- The middle classes were very limited.
- The majority belonged to the lower sections, earning very little.
- Food was cheap, Hindus were mostly vegetarian; the Muslims ate meat, wine was used, consumption of opium and *bhang* was also common.
- Amusements included rearing pigeons, dance, music, hunting, chess, polo and kite-flying.
- The position of women was bad, both among Muslims and Hindus.
- Among Hindus, *Sati* and child marriage were prevalent, but not widow remarriage.
- There was mutual tolerance between Hindus and Muslims during Akbar's reign and Sanskrit books were translated into Persian. Indians learnt Persian and Arabic. But the relations deteriorated after the death of Akbar.
- Social evils included superstitions, very low position of women, dowry system, drinking, gambling, etc.

Art, Architecture and Literature

- The Mughal emperors were very fond of fine arts. Architecture flourished. Use of costly materials and beautification, minarets and domes became common.
- In painting, naturalistic themes were used; there was a growth of Rajput and Kangra schools.
- Persian, Hindi and Sanskrit literature flourished;

Kabir, Birbal, Surdas, Bhushan, etc., were great writers of the time.

- Education was not the duty of the state, but the rulers encouraged it. Female education was ignored.

Bhakti Movement

- It was a national socio-religious movement spread in the middle ages in India.
- It aimed at the rapprochement between Hindus and Muslims.
- The Chief exponents of the Bhakti Movement were Ramanuja (pioneer) in the South, Ramanand and Kabir in Uttar Pradesh, Namdev in Maharashtra, Chaitanya in Bengal and Guru Nanak Dev in Punjab.

Sufism

- A form of mysticism on which there was influence of Buddhist and Hindu yogic practices.
- Its important exponents were Khwaja Moin-ud-din Chisti of Ajmer, Sheikh Nizam-ud-din Aulia and Nasir-ud-din of Delhi, Sheikh Salim Chisti of Sikri and Farid-ud-din Gang-Shakar.

LATER HINDU DYNASTIES

Kingdom of Vijayanagar (1336-1565 AD)

- It was the last great Hindu kingdom of southern India founded by Harihara and Bukka brothers in 1336 AD.
- During the rule of this dynasty, Hinduism (both *Vaishnavism* and *Saivism)* was revived.

- During the reign of Deva Raya I, the Italian traveller Nicolo Conti visited in 1420.
- The greatest rulers of this dynasty were Deva Raya II and Krishnadeva Raya (1509-1530).
- During the reign of Deva Raya II, the Persian traveller Abdul Razak visited in 1443.
- Krishnadeva Raya was a successful warrior. He was on friendly terms with the Portuguese who imported horses and foreign goods for him.
- He was a great patron of arts and learning.
- In 1565, the Deccan sultanates fought and defeated Ramaraya, the ruler of Vijayanagar in the famous Battle of Talikota (near Banihatti), which destroyed once and for all the chances of Hindu supremacy in the South. Ramaraya was killed in the battle.
- The main reason for the defeat of Ramaraya was unity among the Muslim rulers.

The Marathas (1649-1708 AD)

- Shivaji (1627-1680) was the founder of the Maratha kingdom.
- He considered it his mission to liberate India from Muslim rule.
- At a very early age, he conquered the forts of Torna, Raigarh, Purandar, etc. Soon he was powerful enough to begin a campaign against Mughal rulers.
- Shivaji was a brave general and an efficient administrator.
- The Maratha method of warfare was guerrilla warfare.

The Peshwas (1713-1857 AD)

- The Peshwa dynasty was founded by *Balaji Vishwanath* (1713-20) who was their ablest ruler and streamlined administration. They aspired for India's sovereignty. Baji Rao I extented the Maratha rule across Northwest india and raided Mughal Delhi. The Maratha rule over Northern India came to an end after the battle with Ahmed Shah Abdali in Panipat in 1761.
- Thus, the scene was left free for the East India Company.

The Sikhs

- Sikhism was started as a religious sect but became a military community with the passage of time.
- *Guru Nanak Dev* (1469-1539) founded the Sikh faith which lays emphasis on unity of God, rejection of casteism and rituals, and brotherhood of man.
- *Guru Gobind Singh* (1666-1708) transformed the religious sect to a military brotherhood.
- It was the martyrdom of *Guru Arjan Dev* in Jahangir's reign which was a turning point in Sikh history, making them enemies of the tyranny of Mughals.
- After Banda Bairagi, the Sikhs lacked effective leadership and they took refuge in the Himalayan hills.
- They formed *misls,* or groups which established independent kingdom in Punjab in the 18th century under Maharaja Ranjit Singh.

THE BRITISH PERIOD

Coming of the Europeans

- The Portuguese were the first to discover a sea route

to India which was free from the Turkish attacks.

- *Vasco-da-Gama* rounded the Cape of Good Hope and landed at Calicut in 1498. The Portuguese soon established a political power along the western coast.
- Albuquerque (1509-1515) was their ablest viceroy.
- The first viceroy was *Francis Almeida* (1505-1509).
- The Dutch Trading Company came in 1602 but their power was not lasting. *Masulipatnam* was associated with them.
- The French founded Pondicherry (now Puducherry) in 1674 and held power till 1763.

The East India Company

- The English East India Company was formed in 1600 by a charter to trade with India.
- In 1612, they built a factory at Surat with Jahangir's permission.
- They had to face Dutch and French opposition in the beginning, but they overcame them successfully .
- The Company's functions expanded to political ambitions.
- Robert Clive led the English forces to capture Arcot and other regions in 1751. Robert Clive was instrumental in laying the foundation of the British empire in India.
- In the Carnatic Wars (three battles between the French and the English), the English finally defeated the French in the Battle of Wandiwash (1760) to gain control over South India.
- In the *Battle of Plassey* (1757), Clive led the Company's forces against Siraj-ud-daula (the Nawab of Bengal)

and defeated him with the help of a conspiracy with Mir Jafar.

- One of the causes of this battle was *Black Hole Tragedy.* It is said that on June 20,1756, Nawab Siraj-ud-daula of Bengal captured Calcutta and imprisoned 146 English prisoners in a small dungeon. It was a hot, sultry night and when the door was opened the next morning, only 23 of them came out alive. Battle of Plassey proved the first step towards the territorial supremacy.
- The *Battle of Buxar* (1764) finally put the Company forces firmly in power.
- In this battle, Clive's forces defeated the conspiracy of Mir Kasim, Shah Alam II and the Nawab of Oudh.
- The main reason for the success of the British was their naval supremacy.

GOVERNOR GENERALS OF INDIA

Warren Hastings (1773-1785)

- He introduced several reforms, established civil and criminal courts and courts of appeal.
- He passed *The Regulating Act, 1773,* giving a legalised working constitution to the Company's dominions in India.
- It envisaged a council of ministers under the Governor-General.
- *The Pitts' India Act of 1784* put the Company's affairs in permanent control of the British Parliament.

Lord Cornwallis (1786-1793)

- He introduced a new revenue system under the *Permanent Settlement of Bengal* in 1793.

- According to the Permanent Settlement, *Zamindars* were declared permanent masters of land and cultivators as their tenants and the revenue to be paid by *Zamindars* was fixed.
- This system was applicable to Bengal and Bihar (which was at that time part of Bengal).
- In the third Anglo-Mysore War (1790-92), Tipu Sultan was defeated. Lord Cornwallis introduced *Civil Services* in India.

Sir John Shor (1793-1798)

- The Charter Act, 1793 was passed by the British Parliament during his reign.
- He built the Sanskrit College at Varanasi.

Lord Wellesley (1798-1805)

- He made an alliance with the Nizam.
- Tipu Sultan was defeated and killed in the Fourth Mysore War (1799).
- Wellesley prepared the *Subsidiary System of Alliances.*
- In this system, the Indian states joining it became the British protectorates and lost their sovereignty and retained authority only on the internal administration in return for British protection.

Sir John Barlow (1805-1807)

- He followed the policy of non-intervention strictly.
- He tried to restore peace with Scindhia and Holkar.

Lord Minto (1807-1813)

- He signed the Treaty of Amritsar in 1809 with Maharaja Ranjit Singh, defining the latter's boundaries to the west of the Sutlej.

- During his period, monopoly of Indian trade of East India Company was abolished by the Charter Act of 1813.

Marquess of Hastings (1813-1823)

- Reforms included introduction of *Ryotwari System,* special attention to education, building of roads, bridges and canals.
- Under *Ryotwari System* (associated with Thomas Munro), the tillers were put under direct contact with the government.
- Final defeat of Maratha confederation came during his time by the Fourth Maratha War (1817-18).

Lord Maherest (1823-1828)

- The chief event during the period was the First Burmese War (1824-26).

Lord William Bentinck (1828-1835)

- He is famous for *social reforms,* such as abolition of Sati (1829), suppression of *Thugee,* suppression of female infanticide and human sacrifices.
- Indians were employed at high posts but on lower salaries.
- Law courts were reformed.
- He also made a treaty with Maharaja Ranjit Singh, the Sikh ruler of Punjab.
- In 1833, with the *Charter Act,* the Company ceased to be a trading company and became administrative.
- The Governor of Bengal was termed the Governor General of India and it was declared that no Indian could be debarred from holding any post under the Company on racial grounds.

- In 1835, English was introduced as the medium of instruction on the recommendations of *Lord Macaulay.*

Sir Charles Metcalfe (1835-1836)

- He is notable for removing restrictions on the press.

Lord Auckland (1836-1842)

- His tenure of office was marked by the *First Afghan War* (1839-42) which caused the greatest misfortune in his career.

Lord Ellenborough (1842-1844)

- He brought the Afghan War to an end and the honour and might of the British were vindicated by a successful expedition to Kabul.
- His short regime was marked by two high-handed acts of injustice, the annexation of Sindh (1843) and the coercion of Scindhia into a humiliation treaty.

Lord Dalhousie (1848-1856)

- In 1849, the *Second Sikh War* (1848-49) was fought in which the Sikhs were defeated by treachery and Punjab was annexed.
- *The Second Burmese War* (1852) resulted in the English getting control of the whole coastline from Chittagong to Singapore.
- Dalhousie rigidly followed the *Doctrine of Lapse* through which the British would get those states whose rulers died without a son to inherit.
- He annexed Satara, Jhansi, Jaipur, Bagpet, Udaipur and Nagpur by applying this doctrine.
- Lord Dalhousie abolished titles and pensions of the native rulers. He annexed Berar and Oudh (which was an act of aggression).

- The *Charter Act of 1853* paved the way for the Crown to take over administration of India.
- It also set up the first Legislative Council at the Centre.
- Reforms included setting up of *PWD*, improvement of *Posts and Telegraphs* on modern lines, laying *first Railway line (1853)*, giving special attention to education and passing the *Widow Remarriage Act (1856)*.
- During his time, postal stamps were issued for the first time.

The Mutiny of 1857

- The Revolt of 1857 (also called the First War of Indian Independence) arose out of a combination of political, economic and socio-religious causes.
- It took place when Lord Canning was the Governor-General.
- The Mutiny was mainly a rebellion of the army.
- The immediate cause was a rumour that cow and pig fat was being used to grease cartridges and this enraged both Hindu and Muslim feelings.
- Political causes included the resentment of Indian rulers about the Doctrine of Lapse, the abolition of titles and pensions.
- Socio-religious and economic causes included the mistreatment of Indians, refusal to give even the deserving Indians good jobs, bad conditions of peasants because of high revenues, taking over of rent-free estates, discontent among the landlords of Oudh.
- The decisive outbreak was at Meerut. Its main leaders were the Rani of Jhansi, Tantya Tope, Nana

Sahab and Bahadur Shah Zafar.

- The Rani of Jhansi was the ablest and the most courageous leader. She was killed while fighting in June 1858.
- The Mutiny failed because it was a premature rising, a localised affair, not a national movement and not well planned; leaders were inexperienced, poor resources, British control over communications and the sea and lack of a definite programme.
- Results of the Munity included transfer of power to the Crown, revocation of the Doctrine of Lapse, re-organisation of the army with proportion of British soldiers increased, religious liberty, growth of national feelings which was soon to lead to the movement for independence.

INDIA UNDER THE CROWN

- The Queen's proclamation on November 1, 1858, transferred the Government of India from the Company to the British Crown. As a result:
- A Viceroy was appointed;
- Princes were given the right to adopt sons;
- Treaties were to be honoured;
- Religious freedom was given to the people;
- Equality of treatment was promised; and
- Progress in every sphere was promised. The proclamation was called the *Magna Carta of Indian Liberties.*

VICEROYS OF INDIA

Lord Canning (1856-1862)

- He was the first Viceroy of India.

- He introduced many reforms. The *Bengal Tenancy Act* improved the position of tenants or farmers.
- The *Indian Penal Code* came into force.
- High courts were established.
- The *Indian Council Act 1861* was the first step towards constitutional government.
- Universities were opened in Calcutta (Kolkata), Madras (Chennai) and Bombay (Mumbai) in 1857.

Lord Elgin (1862-1863)

- His rule saw the *Wahabi* sect of Muslims revolt on the north-western frontier, but was suppressed.

Sir John Lawrence (1864-1869)

- His rule saw the war with Bhutan, famine in Orissa and friendly contacts with Afghanistan.

Lord Mayo (1869-1872)

- His achievement was the decentralisation of finances in India and also making the first Provincial Settlement. In 1871, the *First Census* took place.

Lord Northbrook (1872-1876)

- He suppressed the Kuka Movement.
- He removed the ruler of Baroda.
- He lowered import duties and abolished export duties.

Lord Lytton (1876-1880)

- He held a magnificent *durbar* at Delhi where Queen Victoria was proclaimed the Empress of India.
- The *Durbar* aroused great discontent because of the money wasted, instead of being spent for relief in the Deccan famine.
- A Famine Commission was appointed which

suggested a *Famine Fund* and construction of railways and irrigation works.

- In 1878, the *Vernacular Press Act* restricted the independence of the press.
- The *Indian Arms Act* was another repressive measure.
- The *Second Afghan War* (1878-80) aroused discontent because of the high cost involved.
- He was also associated with *Indianisation of Civil Services* and *Ilbert Bill.*

Lord Ripon (1880-1884)

- He was a liberal statesman who favoured giving a greater share of administration to Indians.
- The *Factory Act* (1881) tried to improve the position of factory workers, prohibited children below twelve from working for more than nine hours a day.
- In 1881, the *Second Census* was conducted.
- The Vernacular Press Act was repealed in 1882. Education was extended.
- The policy of free trade was followed.
- The most constructive work was the enactment of acts regarding *local self-government.*
- The *Ilbert Bill* was passed in 1883, which sought to remove judicial disqualifications on racial distinction.

Lord Dufferin (1884-1888)

- His rule saw the formation of the Indian National Congress in 1885.

Lord Lansdowne (1888-1894)

- His Viceroyalty saw the passing of the second *Indian Councils Act 1892,* by which the functions of the Legislative Councils were enlarged, the members in the Imperial and Provincial Legislative Councils were increased.

Lord Elgin II (1894-1899)

- The Anglo-Russian Convention was signed in 1895, by which Russia recognised the river Oxus as the southern boundary of its empire.
- During 1890-97, a greater part of India was afflicted by famine.

Lord Curzon (1899-1905)

- He was a very able Viceroy and introduced many reforms.
- He laid the strategic railway lines.
- The North West Frontier Province (NWFP) was formed.
- The *financial reforms* included reduction of salt tax.
- The *Police reforms* saw salaries of policemen raised, training schools, and establishment of Criminal Investigation Department (CID).
- The *Agricultural reforms* included the *Punjab Land Alienation Act (1905)* which was useful to the cultivators, establishment of cooperative credit societies, Agricultural Research Institute, agricultural development and improvement in irrigation.
- The *Ancient Monument Preservation Act* (1904) and the founding of the Archaeological Department helped to save ancient historical buildings.
- The famine and plague of 1899-1900 led to the recommendation of more railways, agricultural banks and greater irrigation facilities.
- In 1905, Bengal was partitioned on administrative grounds and it evoked strong criticism of the people.

Lord Minto II (1905-1910)

- He came at a time when the country was full of discontent.
- In 1906, *Muslim League* was formed at Dacca (Dhaka) under Nawab Salimullah Khan of Dacca, although the idea of Pakistan was conceived by Chawdhary Rahmat Ali.
- The Anglo-Russian Convention (1907) was held to counter the common danger from Germany.
- The *Minto-Morley Reforms* (also called Indian Councils Act, 1909) increased the number of elected members of the Central and Provincial Legislative Councils.
- The System of *communal electorates* for Muslims was introduced. The reforms were criticised bitterly.

Lord Hardinge II (1910-1916)

- He held a magnificent *durbar* at Delhi to celebrate the accession of King George V in 1911. Partition of Bengal was annulled.
- Delhi became the new capital.
- When Lord Hardinge made his entry into the assembly, a revolutionary threw a bomb.
- During his Viceroyalty, the *First World War* broke out in 1914. India gave wholehearted cooperation to the Allies.

Lord Chelmsford (1916-1921)

- His Viceroyalty saw the *August Declaration* in 1917 that said that control over the Indian Government would be gradually transferred to the Indian people.
- The *Government of India Act (December 1919),* also called the Montague-Chelmsford Reforms, intro-

duced the system of *Dyarchy* in the provinces. Under this system, a few subjects, which the provinces were empowered to administer, were transferred to the ministers responsible to Provincial Legislative Councils, e.g. education, public health, etc.

- The rest of the subjects were left in the charge of the members of Executive Councils, who were not responsible to provincial legislatures.
- A High Commission for India was appointed.
- The *Rowlatt Act* of March 1919 created great anger among the Indians and was instrumental in leading to Mahatma Gandhi's *Satyagraha* and other protests.
- On April 13, 1919, the *Jallianwala Bagh Massacre* took place under the direction of General Dyer.
- The *Khilafat Movement* began in August 1920 as a protest against the Allies' shabby treatment of Turkey.
- The *Non-Cooperation Movement* was started in September 1920.

Lord Dalhousie (1921-1926)

- His rule saw the visit of the *Prince of Wales* which was boycotted.
- The Non-Cooperation Movement was at its height but was abruptly suspended in 1922 following the violent Chauri-Chaura incident.

Lord Irwin (1926-1931)

- His Viceroyalty saw the appointment of *Simon Commission* and its boycott by the Indians.
- The Congress passed its *Independence Resolution* in 1929.
- Mahatma Gandhi began *Civil Disobedience Movement* in 1930, with the Dandi March to break the salt law.

- In November 1930, the *First Round Table Conference* took place, unattended by Congress representatives.
- Then came the *Gandhi-lrwin Pact (March 1931),* and political prisoners were released.

Lord Willingdon (1931-1936)

- His Viceroyalty saw the *Second Round Table Conference* in December 1931 attended by Mahatma Gandhi as the sole representative of the Congress, but it was useless.
- Gandhi was arrested on return from London.
- The *Communal Award* of August 1932 assigned seats to different religious communities and gave separate electorates to the depressed classes.
- The *Poona Pact* in September 1932 between *Hindus* and the *Depressed Classes* agreed upon a practically joint electorate.
- The *Third Round Table Conference* in November 1932 did not prove fruitful.
- The *Government of India Act, 1935* was passed.
- Bihar and Quetta suffered severe earthquakes.

Lord Linlithgow (1936-1943)

- During his Viceroyalty, provincial autonomy was established.
- Congress ministries were established in 1937. When India joined the *Second World War* in 1939 without consulting the Central Legislative Assembly, the Congress ministries resigned as a protest.
- The day was observed as *Day of Deliverance* by the Muslim League under the leadership of Muhammad Ali Jinnah.

- He also made a demand for Pakistan.
- The *Cripps' Mission* in 1942 was a failure.
- The *Quit India Resolution* was passed by the Congress in 1942, as a result of which its leaders were thrown into prison.

Lord Wavell (1944-1947)

- His Viceroyalty saw the end of the Second World War (1945).
- The *Wavell Plan* formulated in June 1945 at *Simla Conference,* was rejected by the Muslim League. The *Cabinet Mission Plan (1946)* provided for an interim government and laid down the procedures for framing the Constitution of India.
- The period is also known for the *Naval Mutiny.*
- Observation *of Direct Action Day* by Muslim League in Calcutta led to riots and bloodshed.
- On February 20, 1947, the British Prime Minister Clement Attlee announced that transfer of power would take place before June 1948.
- Riots and disturbances led to a vigorous demand for the partition of India.

Lord Mountbatten (1947-1948)

- He decided that partition of India was the only way to resolve the political deadlock. His *June 3, 1947 Plan* partitioned the country.
- Indian Independence Act made India and Pakistan dominions, India on August 15, 1947 and Pakistan on the August 14, 1947.
- The State of Kashmir acceded to the Indian Union after the raids engineered by Pakistan.

REVOLUTIONARY MOVEMENTS IN NORTHERN INDIA

- A meeting of revolutionaries form all parts of India was called at Kanpur in October, 1924.
- The Hindustan Socialist Republican Association (HSRA) was founded at Kanpur in Oct., 1924 by Sachindra Nath Sanyal, Jogesh Chandra Chatterjee, Ram Prasad Bismil and Chandra Shekhar Azad.
- They committed a dacoity in a running train on August 9, 1925 at Kakori on the Lucknow-Saharanpur section of the Northern Railway. Four revolutionaries – Ram Prasad Bismil, Asfaqullah Khan, Roshan Lal and Rajendra Lahiri were sentenced to death.
- Bhagat Singh and Batukeshwar Dutt threw two crude bombs in Central Legislative Assembly on April 8, 1929, when the Public Safety Bill and the Trade Disputes Bill were being discussed.
- Bhagat Singh, Sukhdev and Rajguru were hanged till death on March 23, 1931 at Lahore Jail.
- Surya Sen (1930), a revolutionary of Bengal, mastermind behind the raid on Chittagong armoury, was hanged in 1933.
- Chandra Shekhar Azad was surrounded by the police at Alfred Park, Allahabad and killed in an encounter on February 27, 1931.

Freedom struggle in India (Gandhi and afterwards)

- Mahatma Gandhi led Champaran Satyagraha movement in Bihar in 1917.
- Mahatma Gandhi, Vallabhbhai Patel and Indulal Yagnik played an important role in Kheda movement in 1918.

- It was the provocative enactment of the Rowlatt Act in February, 1919 which made Gandhi launch an all-India Satyagraha campaign for the first time.
- The Jallianwala Bagh incident took place on April 13, 1919, in which 379 innocent people were killed.
- The Non-cooperation Movement (1920-22) was the first all-India movement.
- The all-white Simon Commission (1927-28) was boycotted by Indians.
- The Nehru Report, finalised at Lucknow in 1928, was drafted by Motilal Nehru and Tej Bahadur Sapru. It formulated a Dominion Status for India.
- The Lahore Congress under the presidentship of Jawaharlal Nehru in 1929 adopted the 'Purna Swaraj' instead of a Dominion Status. The Civil Disobedience Movement (1930-32) was led by Mahatma Gandhi. Gandhi started the Dandi March (March 12 to April 6, 1930) from Sabarmati Ashram to the Sea-coast).
- The Karachi session of the Congress (1931) endorsed the Gandhi-Irwin pact. In the second Round Table Conference (1931), Gandhi represented the Congress alone. The August offer (1940) disappointed Gandhi and then Congress started individual Satyagraha. The proposals of Cripps' Mission (1942) were rejected by the Congress and it started Quit India Movement on August 9, 1942.
- The Cabinet Mission under the presidentship of Sir Stafford Cripps (1946) presented a formula of dividing India into three groups, which was rejected by Indian people.
- The Mountbatten Plan (1947) became the basis of partition and independence of India which was ratified by the British Parliament and Crown on July 18, 1947, and implemented on August 15, 1947.

2

INDIAN POLITICS

CONSTITUTIONAL HISTORY OF INDIA

- The Regulating Act of 1773: Established a Supreme Court at Calcutta and Elijah Impey was appointed the Chief Justice.
- The Pitt's India Act of 1784: Distinguished between commercial and political function of the company.
- The Charter Act of 1793: Salaries of the members of the board to be drawn from the Indian exchequer.

The Charter Act of 1813

- Company's monopoly over trade was abolished in India but its monopoly over trade with China and for trade in tea was retained.
- This Act asked the company to spend one lakh rupees every year on education in India.

The Charter Act of 1833

- The Governor-General of Bengal was henceforth to be styled as the Governor-General-in-Council.
- The Governor-General-in-Council was empowered to make laws and regulations.
- The council was enlarged for the purpose of

legislative work by the addition of the fourth member known as the law member (who had no voice in executive matters).

The Charter Act of 1853

- Took a decisive step in separating the legislative machinery from executive.
- The Act created a separate Legislative Council for India consisting of 12 members.
- The council of Governor-General was enlarged for legislative purposes by the addition of 6 new members.

The Government of India Act, 1858

- Transferred legislative power of the Government of India from the East India Company to the British Crown.
- The *Dual Government* introduced by Pitt's Act was abolished by this Act.
- The Powers of the Crown were exercised by the secretary of state for India assisted by a council of 15 members, known as *the Council of India.*

The Indian Council Act of 1861

- It brought about the beginning of the representative institution.
- Indians were associated with the work of legislation for the first time.

The Indian Council Act of 1892

- It increased the number of members in the central and provincial councils.
- Introduced the election system partially.
- Enlarged the functions of the council.

The Indian Council Act, 1909 (Morley-Minto Reforms)

- The number of additional members in the Governor-General's Council was raised from 16 to 60.
- Muslims were given separate representation.
- The principle of election was introduced, but only in some cases.

The Government of Indian Act, 1919

(Montague-Chelmsford Reforms)

- In matters of legislation, subject were divided into centre and provinces.
- Separate representation was given to Sikhs, Christians, Anglo-Indians, etc.
- For the first time, Indian Legislative Council was made Bicameral (two houses).

The Goverment of India Act, 1935

- The Act provided for the establishment of an *All India Federation* and new system of government for the provinces on the basis of provincial autonomy.
- Council of State having 260 members was to be permanent house with 1/3 members to retire every two years.
- Federal Assembly having 5 years duration consisted of 375 members.

The Indian Independence Act, 1947

- This Act called for the two Dominions, namely, India and Pakistan.
- It asked for power to be transferred to the Indians on August 15, 1947.

Constitutional Development

- In 1935 the Indian National Congress demanded a Constituent Assembly to frame the Constitution.
- In 1938, Jawaharlal Nehru, on behalf of the Congress declared that the Constitution of free India must be framed, without outside interference, by a Constituent Assembly elected on the basis of adult franchise.
- The demand was accepted by British Government during *August offer 1940.*
- In 1942, (Cripps' Mission) Sir Stafford Cripps, a member of the cabinet came to India with a draft proposal of British Government on the framing of an Independent Constitution.
- The Cabinet Mission was sent to India on May 16,1946. The British Parliament conceded India's demand to set up a Constituent Assembly which was to draft its own constituent.

Framing of the Constitution

- The Drafting committee of Constituent Assembly was set up on August 29, 1947. It consisted of seven members, including a Chairman.
- The Constituent Assembly which had been elected by indirect election by the members of the provincial Legislative Assemblies (Lower House only) held its first sitting on December 9, 1946; reassembled on August 14 , 1947.
- The Drafting Committee assembled under the Chairmanship of Dr. B.R. Ambedkar.
- On 26 November, 1949, the Constitution received the signature of the President of the Assembly and was declared passed.

- January 26, 1950 is the date of the implementation of the Indian Constitution.

The Preamble

- Indian Constitution starts with a Preamble which outlines the main objectives of the Constitution.
- The Preamble was drafted and moved by Pandit Jawaharlal Nehru.
- The words socialist, secular, and integrity were added in the Preamble by the 42nd Amendment Act, 1976.
- The Preamble to the Indian Constitution reads thus: "We, the people of India, having solemnly resolved to constitute India into a *Sovereign, Socialist, Secular, Democratic Republic* and to secure to all its citizens: Justice, social, economic and political;

  Liberty of thought, expression, belief, faith and worship;

  Equality of status and of opportunity;

  and to promote among them all

  Fraternity assuring the dignity of the individual and the unity and integrity of the Nation;

  In our Constituent Assembly this twenty-sixth day of November, 1949, do hereby adopt, enact and give to ourselves this Constitution."

NATURE OF INDIAN CONSTITUTION

Important Features

- The Constitution of India provides for a federal system of government.

- Article 1 of the Constitution describes India as a 'Union of States'.
- "Federalism is a system of government in which all the administrative powers are divided between the Central and the State Governments by the Constitution, and both are supreme within their respective spheres. The State Governments are neither agents of the Central Government nor do they draw their authority from it. On the other hand, both the Central and State Governments draw their authority from the Constitution."
- The original Constitution is a written document containing 395 Articles and eight Schedules.
- The Supreme Court of India, which is the apex court in India, acts as the custodian of the Constitution.
- All the powers have been divided into three lists- the Union List (99 items), the State List (61 items) and the Concurrent List (52 items).
- In case of clash between the Central and State laws, the former prevails.
- The residuary powers have been vested by the Constitution in the Central Government.
- The Constitution of India stands at the top of the hierarchy of all laws, both Central and State.

Unitary Features

- In the division of powers, 99 items have been included in the Union List, while the State List contains only 61 items.
- Both the Centre and the States have power to legislate, but the Central Government enjoys an over-riding position.

- The States in India have not been given any right to make or unmake their own Constitutions. The framers provided a single, common and unified Constitution, both for the Centre and the States.
- The Indian Constitution, creates a single Citizenship of India which is common to all the people of various States and Union Territories.
- The Indian Constitution accords representation to the various states in the Rajya Sabha on the basis of their population.
- During the proclamation of Emergency, the Parliament gets the power to legislate for the whole or any part of the territory of India.
- Under the Indian Constitution, the Governors, who are the administrative heads of the State administration, are appointed by the President and hold office during his pleasure.
- In Indian Constitution, there is the provision of common All India Services like IAS, IPS, etc.
- The members of these services are appointed by the President of India on the recommendations of the Union Public Service Commission.
- The judges of High Courts are also independent of the States, which do not possess any power with regard to their appointment, removal and service conditions. They are appointed by the President and can be removed by him.

Parts of the Indian Constitution

- Part I – State and Union territories
- Part II – Citizenship
- Part III – Fundamental Rights

- Part IV – Directive Principles of State Policy
- Part V – The Union
- Part VI – The States
- Part VII – The States in Part B of the First Schedule
- Part VIII – Administration of Union territories
- Part IX – The Panchayats
- Part IX – A: The Municipalities
- Part IX – B: The Co-operative Societies
- Part X – Provisions for SCs/STs
- Part XI – Relations between the Union and the States
- Part XII – Finance, Property, Contracts and Suits
- Part XIII – Trade, Commerce and Inter-course within the territory of India
- Part XIV – Services under the Union and the States
- Part XIV – A: Tribunals
- Part XV – Elections
- Part XVI – Special provisions relating to certain classes
- Part XVII – Official language
- Part XVIII – Emergency provisions
- Part XIX – Miscellaneous
- Part XX – Amendment to the Constitution
- Part XXI – Temporary, Transitional and Special Provisions
- Part XXII – Short Title, Commencement, Authoritative Text in Hindi and Repeals.

Schedules of the Constitution

- **First Schedule:** It belongs to the list of States and Union Territories. There are 28 States and 7 Union Territories.

- **Second Schedule:** It deals with the salaries and allowances of the President, Vice-President, Chief Justice of Supreme Court, High Court, the Speaker of Lok Sabha, Comptroller and Auditor General of India, etc.
- **Third Schedule:** It deals with forms of oaths or affirmations.
- **Fourth Schedule :** It details the allocation of seats in Rajya Sabha per state or Union Territory.
- **Fifth Schedule:** It deals with administration and control of Scheduled Areas and Scheduled Tribes
- **Sixth Schedule:** It deals with provision of administration of tribal areas in Assam, Maghalaya, Tripura, Mizoram and Arunachal Pradesh.
- **Seventh Schedule:** It deals with allocation of powers and functions between Union and States. It contains 3 lists: *(a) Union List; (b) State List; and (c) Concurrent List.*
- **Eighth Schedule:** It contains twenty-two languages of India recognised by the constitution. These are listed below:

  1. Assamese; 2. Bengali; 3. Gujrati; 4. Hindi; 5. Kannada; 6. Kashmiri; 7. Konkani; 8. Malayalam; 9. Manipuri; 10. Marathi; 11. Nepali; 12. Oriya; 13. Punjabi; 14. Sanskrit; 15. Sindhi; 16. Telugu; 17. Tamil; 18. Urdu; 19. Bodo; 20. Dogri; 21. Santhali; 22. Maithili.
- **Ninth Schedule:** It has been added by the 1st Amendment in 1951. It contains acts and orders related to land tenure, road tax, railways and industries.
- **Tenth Schedule:** It has been added by the 52nd Amendment in 1985. It contains provisions for dis-

qualification of the Members of the Parliament and State Legislature on the ground of defection.

- **Eleventh Schedule:** It has been added by the 73rd Amendment Act, 1992. It contains a list of subjects on which schemes may be entrusted to the Panchayats by the Legislative Assembly of a State for implementation (Panchayati Raj).
- **Twelfth Schedule:** It has been added by the 74th Amendment Act, 1992. It contains the list of subjects on which schemes may be entrusted to Municipalities by the Legislative Assembly of a State for implementation.

STATES AND UNION TERRITORIES

- Part I, First Schedule (Article 1 to 4) of Constitution deals with the Union and its Territory.
- *Article 1* of Constitution says: "India, that is Bharat, shall be a Union of States."
- *Article 3* deals with the formation of new states out of the territory of the existing States.

Re-organisation of States

- With the dextrous efforts of Sardar Vallabhbhai Patel, the Princely States and British Indian provinces were merged, but the demand to formulate new States on linguistic basis gained currency which culminated into the creation of Andhra Pradesh on November 1, 1953.
- Later, Fazal Ali Commission's recommendation led to the formation of State Reorganisation Act, 1956.
- It created 14 States and 6 Union Territories.

Special Status to Jammu & Kashmir

- The Indian Constitution accords special status to the state of Jammu & Kashmir.
- Article 1 of Indian Constitution refers Jammu & Kashmir as the part of the territory of India-as fifteenth state.
- Under Art. 370, the power of the Parliament to make laws for the State shall be limited to those matters in the Union and Concurrent list which are in concurrence with the government of the State. A *separate Constitution* was created for Jammu & Kashmir by a Constituent Assembly appointed by the State and came into force from January, 26, 1957.

STATES AND UNION TERRITORIES

State	Capital
Andhra Pradesh	Hyderabad
Arunachal Pradesh	Itanagar
Assam	Dispur
Bihar	Patna
Chhattisgarh	Raipur
Goa	Panaji
Gujarat	Gandhinagar
Haryana	Chandigarh
Himachal Pradesh	Shimla
Jammu & Kashmir	Srinagar (summer) Jammu (winter)
Jharkhand	Ranchi

Karnataka	Bangalore
Kerala	Thiruvananthapuram
Madhya Pradesh	Bhopal
Maharashtra	Mumbai
Manipur	Imphal
Meghalaya	Shillong
Mizoram	Aizwal
Nagaland	Kohima
Orissa	Bhubaneshwar
Punjab	Chandigrah
Rajasthan	Jaipur
Sikkim	Gangtok
Tamil Nadu	Chennai
Tripura	Agartala
Uttarakhand	Dehradun
Uttar Pradesh	Lucknow
West Bengal	Kolkata

UNION TERRITORIES

1. Andaman & Nicobar Island	Port Blair
2. Chandigarh	Chandigarh
3. Dadra & Nagar Haveli	Silvassa
4. Daman & Diu	Daman
5. Delhi	Delhi

6. Lakshadweep Kavaratti
7. Pudducherry Pudducherry

CITIZENSHIP, FUNDAMENTAL RIGHTS, DUTIES AND DIRECTIVE PRINCIPLES

CITIZENSHIP

- Part II (Articles 5 to 11) contains provisions relating to citizenship of India.
- The Constitution of India provides for a single citizenship for the whole of India and the provisions for opting Indian citizenship are as follows:
  - Domicile: A person domiciled in India at the commencement of the Constitution of India is a citizen of India provided:
    - He was born in India.
    - Either of his parents was born in India.
    - He has ordinarily been resident in India for the last five years immediately preceding the commencement of the Constitution.
  - Immigrants from Pakistan: Any person who has migrated to India from Pakistan is a citizen of India provided he or either of his parents or grandparents were born in pre-partition India.
  - If he migrated before July 19, 1948, he has been registered as a citizen.
- **Migrants to Pakistan:** A migrant to areas now forming Pakistan after March 1, 1947 is a Citizen of India.
- **Residents in Foreign Countries:** Any person ordinarily residing out of India is deemed to be citizen of India if he or either of his parents or any of his grandparents

was born in pre-partition India, provided that he is registered as citizen by a diplomatic or consular representative of India.

Acquisition of Citizenship

- According to the Citizenship Act, 1955, citizenship could be acquired through any of the following methods:
- **By Birth:** All the persons born in India on or after January 26, 1950 are treated as citizens by birth.
- **By Descent:** A person born even outside India shall be treated as a citizen of India by descent if at the time of his birth, his father is a citizen of India.

Loss of Citizenship

- The Citizenship Act envisages the following three methods for the loss of the Indian citizenship:
    - By Renunciation
    - By Termination
    - By Deprivation
- It is noteworthy that the citizenship of a person can be taken from him only if he has acquired Indian citizenship by naturalisation, pure domicile or registration.
- Persons who are citizens of India by birth or descent, cannot be deprived of their citizenship in any of the above manners.

FUNDAMENTAL RIGHTS

- Part III (Articles 12 to 35) of the Constitution dealing with Fundamental Rights constitutes the Magna Carta of the essential freedoms of the Indian people.

- These rights are justiciable and can be enforced by courts, if necessary.
- Originally, these were seven but in 1979, through the 44th Amendment, the Right to Property was removed.
- Fundamental Rights are those rights which are essential for the growth of an individual's personality and are enjoyed by every citizen, irrespective of caste, colour, creed, race and sex.
- Indian Constitution guarantees the following Fundamental Rights:

Right to Equality ***(Art. 14 to 18)***

- Equality before law;
- Prohibition of discrimination by the State on the grounds of religion, caste, sex or place of birth;
- Equality of opportunity in matters of public appointment;
- Abolition of untouchability; and
- Abolition of titles, except military and academic distinctions.

Right to Freedom ***(Art. 19 to 22)***

- This group guarantees to all citizens freedom of speech and expression, association, movement, residence, assembly, profession, etc.

Right against Exploitation ***(Art. 23 to 24)***

- Prohibition of traffic in human beings and forced labour.
- Prohibition of employment of children below the age of 14 years in factories, mines and hazardous jobs.

Right to Freedom of Religion ***(Art. 25 to 28)***

- Freedom of conscience and right to profess, practice and propagate religion.
- Freedom to manage religious affairs.
- Freedom as to the payment of taxes for promotion of any particular religion.
- Immunity from attendance at religious instructions of worship in educational institutions.

Cultural and Educational Rights ***(Art. 29 to 30)***

- Protection of language, script or culture of minorities.
- Right of minorities to establish and administer educational institutions.
- Prohibition of denial of admission into any educational institution maintained by the State or receiving aid out of State funds on account of religion, race, caste or language.

Right to Constitutional Remedies (***Art. 32)***

- This article provides for the enforcement of above rights through the judicial writs of *habeas corpus, mandamus, prohibition, quo warranto* and *certiorari.*
- **Habeas Corpus:** It is issued against wrongful detention and the detained person is released after his innocence is proved. This cannot be issued in the case of criminal offence.
- **Mandamus:** It is issued to lower court, tribunal or a public official to perform his duties through which Fundamental Rights of a person are enforced.
- **Prohibition:** It forbids a lower court to perform an act which is outside its jurisdiction.

- **Quo Warranto:** It restrains a person from acting in a public office to which he is not entitled.
- **Certiorari:** It is issued when a court or tribunal acts beyond its jurisdiction. If differs from prohibition in that it is issued after the act is performed.

FUNDAMENTAL DUTIES

Ten Fundamental Duties were incorporated in the Constitution under Art. 51A through the 42nd Amendment in 1976. These are following:

- To abide by the Constitution and respect its ideals and institutions, the National Flag and the National Anthem.
- To cherish and follow the noble ideals which inspired our national struggle for freedom.
- To uphold and protcet the sovereignty, unity and integrity of India.
- To defend the country and render national service when called upon to do so.
- To promote harmony and the spirit of common brotherhood amongst all the people of India transcending religious and linguistic differences.
- To renounce practices derogatory to the dignity of women.
- To value and preserve the rich heritage of our composite culture.
- To protect and improve the natural environment including forests, lakes, rivers and wildlife, and to have compassion for living creatures.
- To develop the scientific temper, humanism and the spirit of inquiry and reform.

- To safeguard public property and abjure violence.
- To strive towards excellence in all spheres of individual and collective activity, so that the nation constantly rises to higher levels of endeavour and achievement.
- To provide primary education to children as a social responsibility (By 86th constitutional amendment).

DIRECTIVE PRINCIPLES

- **Part IV (Article 36-51):** deals with the provision of the directive principles with the aim of ensuring a just and equitable socio-economic order (welfare state). These are not enforceable by the court.
- **Article 36:** to secure and protect a social order.
- **Article 38:** responsibility securing a social order permitted by social, economic and political justice.
- **Article 39:** to provide adequate means of livelihood for all citizens, to secure equal pay for equal work for men as well as women.
- **Article 40:** makes it the duty of the State to organise a Village Panchayat as a unit of self-governance.
- **Article 41:** asks the State to secure for its people the opportunity to work, wage and public assistance in case of unemployment, old age, sickness, etc.
- **Article 42:** human condition of work and maternity relief.
- **Article 43:** stands for right to living wage and decent standard to life. It also secures worker's right to participate in management of industries.
- **Article 44:** enjoins upon the State to secure a uniform civil code for citizens.

- **Article 45:** stands for providing free and compulsory primary education.
- **Article 46:** gives emphasis on promoting educational and economic interests to weaker section and protecting them from social injustice.
- **Article 47:** holds that State shall endeavour to raise the level of nutrition and standard of living and improve public health.
- **Article 48:** the State shall organise agriculture and animal husbandry on modern lines.
- **Article 49:** to protect all monuments of historic interest and national importance.
- **Article 50:** enjoins upon the state the duty to separate judiciary from executive.
- **Article 51:** the State shall endeavour to promote international peace and amity.

The New Flag Code

- The amended Flag code came into effect from January 26, 2003.
- One can hoist the flag only form sunrise to sunset.
- The ratio of width to length of the flag should be 2 : 3.
- Don't print on a costume, cushion or napkin either.
- Don't use as a shroud for funerals.
- Don't drape the flag on vehicles.
- Don't hoist it upside down.
- It must not touch the ground.
- It must fly higher than all other flags except that of the UN or other nations.
- Don't fly a damaged flag.

UNION EXECUTIVE

THE PRESIDENT

- The President holds office for a period of five years from the day on which he enters his office.
- He is eligible for re-election.
- The President takes oath in the presence of Chief Justice of India, or in his absence, senior-most Judge of the Supreme Court.
- He can submit his resignation to the Vice-President.

Qualification for Election of President

- He must be a Citizen of India.
- He must have completed the age of 35 years.
- He must be qualified for election as a member of the Lok Sabha.
- He must not hold any office of profit under the Government of India or the Government of any State or under any local authority subject to the control of any of these Governments.

Election of the President

- The President is elected by the members of an electoral college consisting of the elected members to both the Houses of the Parliament and the elected members of the Legislative Assemblies of the States.
- The nominated members of both the houses of Parliament, the nominated members of the State Legislative Assemblies and the members of the State Legislative Council, do not participate in the election of the President.

- The President's election is held in accordance with a system of proportional representation by means of a single transferable vote and the voting is by secret ballot.
- The value of vote of an MLA and MP is such that a true federal character of the office of the President is maintained, by striking a balance between the State and the Centre.
- **Value of the Vote of an MLA**

$$= \frac{\text{Population of the State}}{\text{Total elected Member of the State Legislature}} \div 1000$$

- **Value of the vote of an MP**

$$= \frac{\text{Value of vote of total MLAs of the States and Union Territories}}{\text{Total elected members of the Parliament (LS + RS)}}$$

- Value of the vote of an MLA differs from one State to another.
- To be declared elected to the office of the President, more than 50 percent of the valid votes are required.
- In case of any dispute regarding the election of the President, only the Supreme Court is authorised to intervene in the matter.

Executive Powers

- The President is the executive head of the Sovereign, Socialist, Secular, Democratic Republic of India.

- He is ex-officio Supreme Commander of the armed forces.
- He can declare war and make peace.

The President Appoints:

- The Prime Minister and other Union ministers.
- The Attorney-General of India.
- Comptroller and Auditor-General of India.
- Judges of the Supreme Court and High Courts.
- Ambassadors and other diplomatic representatives.
- The Governor of a State or the Lieutenant-Governor or Chief Commissioner or Administrator of a Union Territory.
- Chairman and members of UPSC and Joint Commission for a group of States.
- Chief Election Commissioner and other members of the Election Commission, Chairman and members of the Finance Commission, Deputy Chairman and members of the Planning Commission, Commission on official language, Commissions for Scheduled Castes and Scheduled Tribes, Commission to investigate the condition of Backward Classes and special officer for linguistic minorities.

Legislative Power

- A bill passed by the Parliament must receive his assent before it becomes an Act, except in the case of Money Bills on which his prior assent is necessary.
- The President enjoys *Veto Power* usually called *pocket veto;* it can be used for withholding a bill for any period of time [Art. 111].
- The President can issue an ordinance when the Parliament is not in session.

- He nominates 12 members to the Rajya Sabha and 2 Anglo-Indian members to the Lok Sabha.
- He can address either House of the Parliament.
- He is an integral part of the Parliament but he himself is not a Member of the Parliament.
- He can summon and prorogue either House of the Parliament, call joint sittings of both Houses, when necessary.
- He can dissolve the Lok Sabha and order fresh elections.

Financial Power

- He causes the annual Union Budget and important reports to be laid before the Parliament.
- No Money Bill can be introduced in the Parliament without his prior consent.
- He appoints a Finance Commission after every five years for allocation of share of proceeds of taxes between the Union and the States.

Judicial Powers

- He can grant pardon, reprieve, respite or remission of punishment or suspend, remit or commute the sentence including the sentence of death.
- The President is the only authority to grant pardon in case of death sentence on the advice of Council of Ministers.
- He is not answerable to any court of law.

Emergency Power

- The President can suspend the whole Constitution or some articles of it under Emergency condition arising out of:

- *National Emergency [Art. 352]:* Due to external aggression or armed rebellion.
- *State Emergency [Art. 356]:* Due to failure of Constitutional machinery in the State.
- *Financial Emergency [Art. 360]:* Due to financial instability or crisis in any region of the country.

Impeachment (Removal) of the President (*Art. 61*)

- The President may be removed from the office by impeachment for the violation of the Constitution.
- The impeachment procedure can be initiated in either House of the Parliament.
- The charge must come in the form of a proposal which must be signed by at least one-fourth of the total membership of that House.
- Before the resolution can be passed, a fourteen days' notice must be given to the President.
- If, after the notice, the House passes the resolution by a majority of not less than two-third members of that House, the matter will be referred to the other House.
- After the changes are framed by one House, the other House investigates them. If found true, the President stands impeached from the date on which such a motion is passed.
- At this time President has the right to defend himself either in person or through his lawyer.

THE VICE-PRESIDENT

- Article 63 provides that there shall be a Vice-President of India.
- Vice-President is elected by the members of two

Houses of the Parliament, in accordance with the system of proportional representation by means of single transferable vote.

- Any dispute relating to or connected with the election of the Vice-President is decided by the Supreme Court whose jurisdiction is exclusive and final.
- The eligibility conditions for election of a person as Vice-President are the same as those for election as President except that for the former, the candidate must be qualified for election as a member of the Council of State (Rajya Sabha).
- The Vice-President is the ex-officio Chairman of the Rajya Sabha.
- When he discharges the functions of the President, the Vice-President shall not perform the duties of the office of the Chairman of Rajya Sabha and shall not be entitled to receive the Salary of the Chairman.

PRIME MINISTER

- The real executive authority is exercised by the Prime Minister and his Council of Ministers.
- The Prime Minister is appointed by the President.
- He gets the same salary as other Ministers.
- He is the ex-officio chairman of the Planning Commission, National Development Council, National Integration Council and Inter-State Council.

Powers

- The President convenes and prorogues all sessions of the Parliament in consultation with him.
- He can recommend the dissolution of Lok Sabha.

- He allocates portfolios, can ask a minister to resign and can get him dismissed by the President.

Council of Ministers

- There are three types of ministers in the Council of Ministers:
  - Minister of Cabinet rank.
  - Minister of State.
  - Deputy Minister: Does not hold separate charge.
- Council of Ministers is collectively responsible to the Lok Sabha.
- It is a team and its members sink or swim together *(Art.* 75). This is called *Collective Responsibility.*
- A person can remain a minister without being a member of either House for up to six months.

UNION LEGISLATURE

- According to Article 79, the Parliament of India consist of the President and two Houses, the *Rajya Sabha (Upper House)* and the *Lok Sabha (Lower House).*

Rajya Sabha

- The Rajya Sabha or the Upper House of Parliament consists of representatives of the States.
- The maximum strength of Rajya Sabha is 250, of which 238 are elected and the remaining 12 are elected by the President for their special contribution to art, literature, science and social service.
- The members of Rajya Sabha are elected for a term of six years.
- Though the Rajya Sabha is a permanent House, one-third of the members retire every two years.

- The elected members of each State Legislature elect their representative on the basis of proportional representation by means of single transferable vote.
- There are no seats reserved for Scheduled Castes and Scheduled Tribes in Rajya Sabha.
- The Deputy Chairman of Rajya Sabha is elected by the members amongst themselves.
- In the absence of the Chairman, the Deputy Chairman presides over the functions and proceedings of the House.
- UP has the largest number of Rajya Sabha Seats (31) and Maharashtra second largest (19), while all the Northeastern States (except Assam) have one seat each.

Powers and Functions

- With regard to legislative powers, the authority of the Rajya Sabha is co-extensive with that of the Lok Sabha.
- No measure can become a law unless it has been passed by the Rajya Sabha.
- As regards Money Bills, these cannot be introduced in the Rajya Sabha.
- When a Money Bill is passed by the Lok Sabha and sent to the Rajya Sabha, the latter can delay the Bill for 14 days. It cannot reject the Bill.

Qualifications for Members of Rajya Sabha

- The candidate must be a citizen of India.
- He must be 30 years of age.
- A resident of the State from which he is seeking election.

Lok Sabha

- The Lok Sabha consists of directly elected representatives.
- There cannot be more than 530 representatives from the States, 20 from the UTs and not more than 2 nominated members from Anglo-Indian community – in total 552.
- At present there are 545 members in the Lok Sabha, of which 530 are from States, 13 from UTs and 2 nominated by the President.
- The representation of Parliament and its number of 543 has been frozen till 2026.
- The party with the largest number of members after the ruling party and having at least one-tenth of the strength of Lok-Sabha is recognised as *opposition party*.
- The leader of opposition in both the Houses of Parliament is entitled to the salary, allowances and other facilities equivalent to that of a Cabinet Minister.

Speaker

- The Speaker – who is the presiding officer of the Lok Sabha – is elected by members amongst themselves.
- The Speaker continues in office even after the dissolution of the Lok Sabha till the newly elected Lok Sabha meets.
- He decides whether a particular Bill is a Money Bill or not and his or her decision is final.
- The Speaker does not vote in the first instance, but exercises vote only to remove a deadlock.
- The majority of the total membership can remove

the Speaker after giving 14 days' notice. (During this time, he doesn't preside over the meeting.)

- After his removal, he continues in office till his successor takes charge.
- The House also elects a Deputy Speaker who discharges the duties of presiding officer in the Speaker's absence.
- Immediately after the Lok Sabha is elected, President appoints a *pro-tem Speaker,* who is the senior-most member in the House.
- He acts as the Speaker till the Speaker is elected by the Lok Sabha.

Tenure

- The constitution provides normal tenure of the Lok Sabha to be 5 years.
- Parliament by 42nd Amendment extended it to 6 years, but the 43rd Amendment Act again restored the original tenure of 5 years.
- The life of Lok Sabha can be extended by the Parliament beyond the five years' term when a proclamation of emergency under Article 352 is in force.

Qualification to be a Member

- The candidate must be a citizen of India.
- He must not be less than 25 years of age.
- He must not be holding any office of profit under the Government.

Session of Parliament

- The maximum gap between two sessions of the Parliament cannot be more than six months.

- It means that the Parliament should meet at least twice a year. However, there are usually three sessions in a year:
  - Budget session (February to May)
  - Monsoon session (July to September)
  - Winter session (November to December)

Joint Session

- A joint session can be ordered by the President to consider a particular bill in question if:
  - A bill passed by one House is rejected by the other.
  - The amendments made by the other house are not acceptable to the House where the bill originated.

END OF THE SESSIONS

Prorogation

- The presiding officer (Speaker) declares the House adjourned *sine die,* when the business of the session is completed.
- Within the next few days the President issues a notification for prorogation of the session.
- The President can also prorogue the Houses while in session.

Adjournment

- This is a short recess within a session of the Parliament called by the presiding officer of the House.
- Its duration may be from a few minutes to days together.

Adjournment *Sine die*

- It is a type of break when the House is adjourned by the presiding officer without fixing any date or time of the next meeting.
- The adjournment does not bring an end of a session, but merely postpones the proceedings.

JUDICIARY

Supreme Court of India

- The Supreme Court consists of a Chief Justice and 30 other judges who are appointed by the President.

Appointment of Judges

- Every Judge of the Supreme Court is appointed by the President by warrant under his hand and seal after consultation with such Judges of the Supreme Court and of the High Courts as the President may consider necessary for the purpose.
- In case of appointment of a Judge, other than the Chief Justice, the Chief Justice of India is to be necessarily consulted.
- A Judge of the Supreme Court remains in office until he attains the age of 65 years.
- The Chief Justice of India gets a salary of ₹ 100,000 per month and other Judges ₹ 90,000 per month.

Qualifications

- A person can be appointed a Judge of the Supreme Court if he has following qualifications:
  - He must be a citizen of India.
  - He has been, for at least five years, a Judge of a High Court or has been, for at least ten years, an

advocate of a High Court or two or more such courts in succession.

- He must be 'in the opinion of the President' a distinguished Jurist.

Composition

- The Supreme Court is the highest Court of Justice in India.
- Its main functions may be studied under the following heads:

Original Jurisdiction:

- The Supreme Court has exclusive jurisdiction in all disputes:
  - between the Government of India and one or more States,
  - between the Government of India and any State or States, and
  - between two or more States.

Advisory Jurisdiction

- The President may refer to the Supreme Court any question of law or fact of sufficient importance for its opinion.
- The President may also refer to the court disputes arising out of any provision of treaty, agreement, covenant, engagement of *sanad,* etc.
- The opinion so expressed is not binding on the President.

Enforcement of Fundamental Rights

- The Supreme Court has been armed with powers to issue directions or orders within the nature of *habeas corpus, mandamus, prohibition, quo warranto* and *certiorari* for the enforcement of the Fundamental Rights conferred by the Constitution.

Custodian of the Constitution

- The authority of the court is further reinforced by the provision that "the law declared by the Supreme Court shall be binding on all courts within the territory of India." (Article 141).

Constitutional Functions of the Supreme Court

Appellate Jurisdiction in matters involving interpretation of constitution

- Article 132 of the Constitution provides that an appeal shall lie to the Supreme Court from any judgement, decree of final orders of the High Court in the territory of India, if the High Court certifies that the case involves substantial question of law as to the interpretation of the Constitution.

Judicial Review of Legislation

- The Supreme Court has also been vested with wide powers in the form of *Judicial Review,* like the Supreme Court of the USA.
- According to the right of judicial review, the Supreme Court can declare any law passed by the Parliament unconstitutional on the ground that it contravenes the provisions of the Constitution.

Independence of Judiciary

- The independence and impartiality of the Supreme Court is the cornerstone of democracy.

HIGH COURT

Appointment of Judges

- A Judge of the High Court is appointed by the President by warrant under his hand and seal after consultation with the Chief Justice of India, the Governor of the State, and in the case of appointment of a Judge other than Chief Justice, the Chief Justice of the High Court is consulted.

Qualifications

A person can be appointed a Judge of a High Court provided he has the following qualifications:

- He is a citizen of India;
- He has, for at least ten years, held a judicial office in the territory of India; and
- He has been the advocate of a High Court for at least ten years of two or more such courts in succession

Conditions of Service

- A Judge of a High Court holds office until he attains the age of 62 years.
- He may be removed from his office in the same manner in which a Judge of the Supreme Court is removed.
- The Chief Justice of a High Court gets a salary of ₹ 90,000 per month and other Judges ₹ 80,000 per month.

STATE EXECUTIVE AND LEGISLATURE

STATE EXECUTIVE : THE GOVERNOR

Appointment

- The Governor of a State, who is the Chief Executive Head of the State, is appointed by the President.
- Only a citizen of India, who has completed 25 years of age, is eligible for appointment as Governor.
- He need not be a resident of that State for appointment as Governor.
- He holds office during the pleasure of the President. Subject to this, he holds office for a period of five years.
- He receives a salary of ₹ 1,10,000 per month.
- During President's Rule, he runs the administration directly with the help of the advisers appointed by the Central Government.

Powers of a Governor

Legislative Powers

- He summons, fixes the time and place for the meeting of the Legislature.
- He addresses the meetings of the legislature at the commencement of the session once in a year.
- Every Bill passed by the legislature must have his assent.
- He has the power to promulgate an ordinance, whenever the legislature is not in session.

Executive Powers

- He appoints the Chief Minister of the State and other ministers on the advice of the Chief Minister.

- He also appoints the Chairman and members of the State Public Service Commission.
- He acts as the agent of the Centre during an Emergency.

Financial Powers

- No Money Bill can be introduced in the Legislative Assembly of the State except on the Governor's recommendation.

Judicial Powers

- He has the power to grant pardons and suspend, remit or commute sentences where the offence is under a law relating to matters within the executive competence of the State.

Discretionary Powers

- He determines whether the Government of a State can or cannot be carried on in accordance with the provisions of the Constitution.
- If he feels that it cannot be so carried on, he can make a report to the President under Article 356 (1).
- The Governor can reserve a bill or bills passed by the State Legislature for consideration of the President.

State Council of Ministers

- The Constitution provides for a Council of Ministers, with a Chief Minister as its head.
- The Governor appoints the Chief Minister and his ministers of the Legislature of the State but sometimes even a non-member may be appointed a minister.

- In that case, he cannot retain his office for more than six months without being a member of the Legislature of the State.
- The Council of Ministers is collectively responsible to the Legislative Assembly of the State.

STATE LEGISLATURE

- The State Legislature consists of the Governor and one or two Houses, as the case may be.
- The Lower House is known as Legislative Assembly (Vidhan Sabha) and the Upper House is known as Legislative Council (Vidhan Parishad).
- The State Legislature of Bihar, Jammu & Kashmir, Karnataka, Maharashtra, Uttar Pradesh and Andhra Pradesh have two Houses each, whereas all other States have only one House each, *i.e.* Vidhan Sabha.

Legislative Assembly

- It is a directly elected body on the basis of adult franchise.
- The total number of members of the Assembly shall in no case be more than 500 or less than 60.
- Like the Lok Sabha, its normal tenure is five years.
- A candidate for election to the Legislative Assembly of a State should be: *(i)* a citizen of India; *(ii)* not less than 25 years of age; *(iii)* not holding an office of profit under the Government; and *(iv)* should possess mental and physical health.

Legislative Council

- Like the Rajya Sabha, it is a permanent body.
- One-third of its members retire after every two years.

- Its total members should not exceed one-third of the members of the State Legislative Assembly.
- Its minimum strength is 40.
- To be eligible for becoming a member of the Legislative Council, a person should possess the same qualification as for becoming a member of the Legislative Assembly.
- However, in respect of age, the minimum age has been fixed at 30 years.

Distribution of legislative powers between the Union and the States

- The Constitution of India makes a division of legislative powers between the Union and the States under the Seventh Schedule.
- There is three-fold distribution of powers between the Union and the States.
- Union List: it includes 99 subjects over which the Parliament has exclusive power of legislation such as Defence, Foreign Affairs, Banking, Currency, etc.
- State List: It comprises 61 items over which the State Legislatures have exclusive powers of legislation, e.g. Health, Agriculture, etc.
- Concurrent List: It comprises 52 items on which the Union and the State Legislatures both can make laws, e.g. criminal law and procedure, marriages, economic planning, education, etc.
- Residuary Powers: According to Article 248 of the Constitution, the residuary powers are vested in the Union Legislature, i.e. the Parliament has the exclusive right to make any law with regard to any matter not specified in the Concurrent of State List.

- Circumstances under which the Parliament may make Laws on a State Subject.

In Normal Times

• The Parliament has the power to make laws with respect to any matter included in the State List for a temporary period, if the Rajya Sabha declares by a two-thirds majority to do so.

During Emergency

• During the proclamation of Emergency or failure of constitutional machinery in a State, the President may assume to himself all or any of the executive powers of the State *[Article 356 (1)]*.

Financial Relations

• Duties levied by the Union but collected and appropriated by the States as Stamp duties.

• Taxes levied and collected by the Union but assigned to the States within which they are leviable as terminal taxes on goods and passengers carried by railways, sea and air.

• Taxes levied and collected by the Union and distributed between the Union and the States as taxes on income other than agricultural income.

PANCHAYATI RAJ

- It aims at taking democracy to the village level by delegating substantial powers to people's organisation.
- It was the main recommendation of Balwant Rai Mehta Committee in order to popularise Community Development Projects and make them more effective.

- It was inaugurated at Nagaur in Rajasthan on October 2, 1959. Later it was introduced in Andhra Pradesh.

Aims and Objectives

- People's participation in government for its success.
- To give shape to the constitutional provisions in Article 40, the Balwant Rai Mehta Committee recommended democratic decentralisation of powers to encourage the introduction of vigorous democratic institutions at the village level.
- Panchayati Raj aims at involving people in development and planning so that dependence on bureaucracy could be reduced.
- The Committee recommended the introduction of a three-tier system of Panchayati Raj:
    - The Gram Panchayat at the village level.
    - The Panchayat Samiti at the block level, with members elected by the panchayat of the villages within the block.
    - The Zila Parishad at the District level.

Gram Sabha

- Though it is not a tier of the Panchayati Raj system, it has a crucial role in making democratic decentralisation complete.
- It is the general body consisting of all the voters residing in the jurisdiction of a Gram Panchayat which extends over one village or a group of villages.
- The Gram Sabha generally meets twice a year.

Gram Panchayat

- The Gram Panchayat is the first tier of the Panchayati

Raj. Its membership usually varies from 6 to 31, all the members being elected by the members of the Gram Sabha by secret ballot.

- The President of the Gram Panchayat is usually known as Sarpanch.

Panchayat Samiti

- The intermediate tier in the Panchayati Raj is known as Panchayat Samiti.
- It is also known as Janpad Panchayat, Taluka Panchayat, Anchalik Panchayat, etc.
- It comprises: (a) Sarpanchas of Panchayats (ex-officio); (b) local MPs, MLAs and MLCs (with or without the right to vote); (c) persons representing women, Scheduled Castes and Scheduled Tribes who are co-opted and whose membership is reserved; and (d) persons representing municipalities, cooperatives, etc.
- The Chairman of this body is a non-official who is elected by the members of the Samiti.

Zila Parishad

- The Zila Parishad constitutes the topmost tier of the Panchayati Raj system.
- It acts as a kind of link between the rural local government Samiti and the State Legislature and Parliament. This is reflected in its composition.
- A Zila Parishad usually consists of the presidents of the Panchayat Samitis in the district.
- Members of Parliament, and Members of State Legislature returned from the district.
- A specified number of representatives of the

Scheduled Castes and Scheduled Tribes and some co-opted members.

- The President of the Parishad is generally elected by the members.
- The District Development Officer is the Chief Executive Officer or the Secretary of the Zila Parishad and the District Officer of various administrative and development departments are its non-voting members.
- In many States, the Collector is associated with the Parishad as a non-voting member.
- The general trend, however, is to exclude the Collector altogether. The term of the Zila Parishad is five years.

Functions of Gram Panchayats

- Promotion of agriculture;
- Rural industries;
- Provision of medical relief;
- Education, primary schools including schools for Scheduled Castes and Scheduled Tribes;
- Maternity, women and child welfare;
- Maintaining common grazing grounds;
- Village roads, tanks and wells;
- Maintenance of sanitation; and
- Execution of other socio-economic programmes.

COMMISSIONS AND OFFICES IN INDIA

Union Public Service Commission (UPSC)

- The Union Public Service Commission (UPSC)

consists of a Chairman and eight other members appointed by the President and they hold office for a period of six years from the date of their appointment. The following are the main functions of the UPSC:

- To conduct examinations for appointment to the services of the Union.
- If requested by two or more States, to assist those States in framing and operating the scheme of joint recruitment for services for which candidates possessing special qualifications are required.
- To serve all or any of the needs of a State with the approval of the President if requested by the Governor of a State.
- To advise the Union Government on all matters relating to methods of recruitment to civil services and for civil posts; suitability of candidates for such appointments, promotions or transfers and any claim for the award of pension for injury sustained by a person while serving under the Government of India.

Attorney-General of India

- The Attorney-General of India is appointed by the President under Article 76 of the Constitution.
- A person qualified to be a judge of the Supreme Court is appointed to the post.
- He is the highest legal adviser to the Government of India and is consulted on all important matters.
- He also appears in the Supreme Court on behalf of the Government of India to conduct important cases.

The main functions of the Attorney-General are:

- To advise the Union Government in legal matters;
- To perform such other legal duties which may be assigned to him by the President; and
- To discharge such other functions conferred on him by or under the Constitution or any other law for the time being in force.
- In pursuance of his duties, the Attorney-General has the right of audience in all courts in the territory of India.
- He has a right to speak or take part in the proceedings in either House of the Parliament or in the joint session of the two Houses or any Committee of the Parliament. He cannot, however, vote.

Comptroller and Auditor-General

- The Comptroller and Auditor-General of India is appointed by the President. His main functions are:
    - To bring into account the receipts and expenditure of the Union Government (except Railways, Defence Services and such other Ministries, the accounts of which are maintained by the departmental authorities);
    - To audit all expenditures from the revenues of the Union and the States;
    - To audit all trading, manufacturing and profit and loss accounts of stores and stocks, where the President may have required him to conduct such audit.
    - The salaries, etc., of the Comptroller are charged

on the Consolidated Fund of India and are thus non-votable.

- The Comptroller and Auditor General of India can be removed from office only after an address of each House of Parliament, supported by a majority of the total membership of that House and not less than two-thirds of the members of the House present and voting.

Backward Classes Commission

- It was set up under the Backward Classes Commission Act, 1993. Its main functions are:
  - To make a proper and effective inquiry for identification of backward classes;
  - To examine complaints of over-inclusion and under-inclusion; and
  - To examine requests for inclusion in the list of backward classes.

Minorities Commission

- It was set up in 1978. Its main functions are:
  - To Safeguard the interests of religious minorities;
  - To Preserve secular traditions;
  - To Promote national integration; and
  - To remove the feeling of inequality and discrimination among minorities.

National Women Commission

- It was set up in 1992.
- Its main function is to investigate and examine legal safeguards provided for women under the

Constitution of India and other laws, and to recommend measures to the Government for their effective implementation.

National Human Rights Commission

- It was established in 1993.
- It deals with complaints of the human rights violations, including excesses by armed forces.

University Grants Commission

- It was set up in 1953. Its main functions are:
  - To promote and coordinate university education;
  - To determine and maintain standards of teaching, examination and research in universities;
  - To inquire into the financial needs of the universities and to make appropriate grants to different universities; and
  - To advise on the establishment of new universities and other matters pertaining to higher education.

3

INTERNATIONAL POLITICS

UNITED NATIONS ORGANISATION (UNO)

- The UN was founded in 1945. The Charter of the UN was signed on June 26, 1945 by representatives of 51 nations who attended the San Francisco Conference.
- The Charter came into force on October 24, 1945.
- The name United Nations was adopted at the suggestion of President Roosevelt (of USA).
- Headquarters of the UN are in New York.

Official Languages

- The Official languages of the UN are English, French, Chinese, Russian, Arabic and Spanish. (The working languages are English and French only).

Aims and Purposes

- The UN is an organisation of nations who have voluntarily joined together to work for world peace. The aims and purposes of the UN are:
- To maintain peace and security in the world.
- To develop friendly relations among nations.

- To work together to remove poverty, disease and illiteracy in the world, and to encourage respect for each other's rights and freedom.
- To be a centre for helping nations to achieve these goals.

Functions

- The UN itself takes measures to end disputes, e.g. by appointing a body of persons to help the opposing sides to agree (as in the case of Arab-Israeli War and Cyprus).
- To take steps to control the situation in the troubled area, the UN sends investigating missions in order to have first-hand information.
- The UN may also take measures to maintain peace if it is threatened and some country has committed an act of aggression, as it did in Korea and in the Congo.
- The UN tries to secure agreement to reduce armaments and work for disarmament. The UN has proclaimed a Universal Declaration of Human Rights and agreed upon a convention to prevent genocide (the killing of groups of people, belonging to a particular race, nationality or religion).

Major Organs

General Assembly

- It is the main deliberative organ of the UN and it expresses the world's views on the work of all the UN organs. All UN members are represented in the General Assembly on an equal basis.
- It meets once a year. Each member can send up to five representatives, but has only one vote.

Security Council

- The Security Council consists of 15 members, each of which has one representative and one vote.
- There are 5 permanent members and 10 non-permanent members.
- The non-permanent members are elected for a 2-year term by a two-thirds majority of the General Assembly.
- The Security Council may look into any dispute or threat to peace brought to its notice.
- It may recommend a peaceful solution or, if necessary, may order the use of force to restore peace.
- It is charged with regulation of armaments and armed forces through the Disarmament Commission.
- It elects, together with the General Assembly, the Judges of the international Court of Justice.
- It recommends the admission of new members, the suspension and/or expulsion of old members and appointment of Secretary General.
- **Veto Power:** Each member has one vote. To pass an important resolution, all five permanent members, plus four others must vote "Yes". If one of the permanent five casts a negative vote, it is called a "Veto" and the resolution stands rejected. In practice, if a permanent member abstains, this is not considered a Veto.

International Court of Justice

- The Court is composed of independent judges, elected regardless of their nationality.
- There are 15 judges; no two of them can be of the same nationality.

- They are elected by the Security Council and the General Assembly of the United Nations sitting independently.
- The judges are elected for a 9-year term and are eligible for immediate re-election.
- The Court sits at the Hague (Netherlands).

The Secretariat

- It is composed of the Secretary-General and some international staff of the UN carrying out its day-to-day operations.
- The Secretary-General is the Chief Administrative Officer. He is responsible for direction of the work of the Secretariat.
- He is appointed as a rule for a five-year term by the General Assembly on recommendation of the Security Council, and may be re-appointed.

International Labour Organisation

- Headquarters-Geneva (Switzerland). Its objects are:
  - To improve labour conditions;
  - To raise the standard of living; and
  - To promote social and economic stability through the joint efforts of government, management and labour.

World Health Organisation

- Headquarters-Geneva. Its objective is the attainment, by all people, of the highest possible standard of health.

International Bank for Reconstruction and Development (World Bank)

- Headquarters-Washington. Its purpose is to lend

money to rebuild wartorn areas and to develop underdeveloped areas.

International Monetary Fund

- Headquarters-Washington. It offers facilities to member nations to expand trade.
- It controls international exchange in order to avoid competitive exchange depreciation.

International Atomic Energy Agency

- The IAEA came into existence on July 29, 1957. It is not a Specialised Agency of the UN. It is an autonomous international organisation under the UN. The purpose of the IAEA is to accelerate and enlarge the contribution of atomic energy for peace, health and prosperity throughout the world and to ensure that any such assistance is not misused for any military purpose. Headquarters – Vienna (Austria).

United Nation International Children's Emergency Fund

- It is a special organisation of the UN originally created to meet the emergency needs of children in Europe after World War II.
- At present, it is a permanent body with a fund, made up of voluntary contributions from governments and individuals, to help children all over the world.
- It works under ECOSOC to help about 90 million children.

WORLD BANK

- The World Bank was set up as a result of the United Nations Monetary and Financial Conference held in July 1944. It is a group of three institutions – the International Bank for Reconstruction and

Development (IBRD) established in 1945; International Finance Corporation (IFC) established in 1956; and the International Development Association (IDA) established in 1960.

- Its chief objectives are: *(i)* assistance to member states for reconstruction and development; *(ii)* to encourage foreign private investment countries; *(iii)* to develop healthy international trade with least possible fluctuation in the balance of payments by assisting the member states in different ways. It advances long-term loans to member-countries for development projects.

WORLD TRADE ORGANISATION

- It is the third pillar of the world's economic system along with IMF and World Bank, with powers to settle disputes between nations and widen the principle of free trade to such sectors as Services and Agriculture. It has 153 members. It came into existence on January 1, 1995.

UN WOMEN

- UN Women is a distinguished organisation dedicated to gender equality and the empowerment of women. This wing was created in July 2010 by the United Nations General Assembly.

CURRENCIES OF COUNTRIES

Afghanistan	Afghani
Algeria	Dinar
Austria	Euro
Bahamas	Bahamian Dollar
Bhutan	Ngultrun

Bahrain	Bahraini Dinar
Bangladesh	Taka
Colombia	Peso
Cuba	Peso
China	Yuan
Egypt	Egyptian Pound
Fiji	Fijian Dollar
Finland	Euro
France	Euro
Germany	Euro
Hungary	Forint
India	Rupee
Indonesia	Rupiah
Italy	Euro
Iran	Rial
Japan	Yen
Jamaica	Jamaican Dollar
Kenya	Kenyan Shilling
Malaysia	Ringgit
Maldives	Maldivian Rufiyaa
Mauritius	Mauritian Rupee
Norway	Norwegian Krone
Nicaragua	Cordoba
Netherlands	Euro
New Zealand	Dollar
Pakistan	Pakistani Rupee
Philippines	Peso

Qatar	Qatari Rial
Romania	Leu
Russia	Ruble
Sweden	Swedish Korne
Sudan	Sudanese Pound
Saudi Arabia	Riyal
Slovakia	Euro
Thailand	Baht
Tonga	Paanga
Turkmenistan	Manat
Togo	Franc CFA
U.K.	Pound
U.S.A.	US Dollar
Ukraine	Hryvnia
UAE	Dirham
Uruguay	New Peso
Uzbekistan	Som
Uganda	Ugandan shilling
Venezuela	Bolivar fuerte
Vietnam	Dong
Vatican City	Euro
Zambia	Kwacha

Largest, Longest, Biggest, Highest and Smallest

Largest Airliner	Boeing 747
Tallest Animal	Giraffe
Fastest Animal	Leopard
Fastest Bird	The Peregrine Falcon

Largest Bird	Ostrich
Smallest Bird	Humming Bird
Longest Railway Bridge	Huey P. Long (U.S.A.)
Tallest Building in Asia	Burj Khalifa Dubai (UAE)
Tallest Standing Structure,	KVLY-TVmast (628.3mt.)
Longest Canal	Beloye (White Sea)
Longest Canal for big ships	Suez Canal (U.A.R.) (161 km)
Longest Canalised System	Volga-Baltic Canal (2960 km)
Highest Capital	Lhasa (Before domination of Tibet by China) 3684 metres above sea-level
Highest City	Wenchua (China); 5,100 metres above sea-level.
Largest Coral Formation	The Great Barrier Reef (North-east coast of Australia)
Largest Creature	Blue Whale
Highest Dam	The Grande (Switzerland)
Largest Desert (world)	Sahara (Africa)
Largest Desert (Asia)	Gobi (Mongolia)
Largest Diamond	The Cullinen (over 11/2 lb.)
Largest Island	Greenland
Deepest Lake	Baikal (Siberia); average depth 701 metres
Highest Lake	Titicaca (Bolivia) 3854 metres above sea level

Largest Fresh Water Lake	Superior (31,200 sq miles)
Largest Salt Water Lake	Caspian Sea (26 metres below sea-level)
Largest Exhibition Ground	Pragati Maiden, New Delhi 150 Acres
Largest Ocean Island	Middle Andaman
Largest River Basin	Ganga Basin
Largest State Library	Moscow Claims to house more than 20,000,000 books
Longest Ropeway in India	Connecting Joshimath in Uttarakhand 4.15 km long
Longest Train in India	Prayag Express running between Delhi and Allahabad 24 bogies
Longest Road Tunnel India	Chiplin-Koya Nager, in Maharashtra, 1 km long
Longest Cave in India	Kremum Kwan Jaintia Hills, Meghalaya
Highest Mountain Range	Himalayas
Longest Mountain Range	Andes (S. America); 8,800 km in length
Largest Museum	American Museum of Natural History, New York city.
Largest Peninsula	Arabia
Hottest Plateau	Arabia
Wettest Place	Mawsynram, India (annual rainfall 11,872mm)
Biggest Planetarium	Tsukuba, Japan
Highest Platform	Pamir (Tibet)

Longest Platform	Khargpur platfrom in West Bengal (India)
Longest Railway	Trans-Siberian Railway (9,600 km long)
Longest River	Nile (6,679 km)
Largest Sea	South China Sea
Brightest Star	Sirius (also called Dog Star)
Tallest TV Tower	Rameshwaram, Tamil Nadu (India, 1000 feet)
Largest Railway Tunnel	Secken Tunnel (Japan)
Longest Wall	Great Wall of China (2400 km)
Greatest Waterfall	Victoria Falls on river Zambesi (Zambia), 1700 metres wide
Highest Waterfall	Angel (Venezuela)

COUNTRIES AND THEIR CAPITALS

Country	**Capital**
Afghanistan	Kabul
Albania	Tirana
Algeria	Algiers
Argentina	Buenos Aires
Armenia	Yerevan
Australia	Canberra
Austria	Vienna
Azerbaijan	Baku
Bahamas	Nassau
Bahrain	Manama
Bangladesh	Dhaka

Barbados	Bridgetown
Belarus	Minsk
Belgium	Brussels
Benin	Contonou (Administrative), Porto Novo (Judicial)
Bhutan	Thimphu
Bolivia	La Paz (Administrative), Sucre (Judicial)
Botswana	Gaborone
Brunei	Bandar Seri Begawan
Bulgaria	Sofia
Burundi	Bujumbura
Cambodia	Phnom Penh
Cameroon	Yaounde
Central Africa	Bangui
Chad	N' Djamena
Chile	Santiago
China	Beijing
Colombia	Bogota
Comoros	Moroni
Congo-Brazzavile	Brazzaville
Costa Rica	San Jose
Cuba	Havana
Cyprus	Nicosia
Czech Republic	Prague
Denmark	Copenhagen
Djibouti	Djibouti city
Egypt	Cairo
Ethiopia	Addis Ababa

Fiji	Suva
Finland	Helsinki
France	Paris
Gabon	Libreville
Georgia	Tbilisi
Germany	Berlin
Ghana	Accra
Greece	Athens
Grenada	St. George's
Guatemala	Guatemala City
Guinea	Conakry
Guyana	Georgetown
Honduras	Tegucigalpa
Hungary	Budapest
India	New Delhi
Indonesia	Jakarta
Iran	Tehran
Iraq	Baghdad
Ireland (or Eire)	Dublin
Israel	Jerusalem
Italy	Rome
Jordan	Amman
Kazakhstan	Astana
Korea (North)	Pyongyang
Korea (South)	Seoul
Laos	Vientiane
Latvia	Riga
Lebanon	Beirut

Lesotho	Maseru
Liberia	Monrovia
Libya	Tripoli
Liechtenstein	Vaduz
Lithuania	Vilnius
Luxembourg	Luxembourg
Macedonia	Skopje
Madagascar	Antanarivo
Mauritania	Nouakchott
Mauritius	Port Louis
Mexico	Mexico City
Monaco	Monaco City
Mongolia	Ulaanbaatar
Morocco	Rabat
Mozambique	Maputo
Myanmar (Burma)	Naypyidaw
Namibia	Windhoek
Nauru	Yaren
Nepal	Kathmandu
Netherlands	Amsterdam
New Zealand	Wellington
Niger	Niamey
Nigeria	Abuja
Norway	Oslo
Oman	Muscat
Pakistan	Islamabad
Philippines	Manila
Poland	Warsaw

Portugal	Lisbon
Qatar	Doha
Romania	Bucharest
Russia	Moscow
Rwanda	Kigali
Senegal	Dakar
Sierra Leone	Freetown
Singapore	Singapore
Slovakia	Bratislava
Slovenia	Ljubljana
Spain	Madrid
Sri Lanka	Colombo
Sudan	Khartoum
Sweden	Stockholm
Switzerland	Bern
Syria	Damascus
Taiwan	Taipei
Tajikistan	Dushanbe
Tanzania	Dar es Salaam (Administrative), Dodoma (Judicial)
Thailand	Bangkok
Turkey	Ankara
Turkmenistan	Ashgabat
UAE	Abu Dhabi
Ukraine	Kiev (Kyiv)
Uzbekistan	Tashkent
Vietnam	Hanoi
Yemen	Sanaa

Zambia	Lusaka
Zimbabwe	Harare

PARLIAMENTS OF COUNTRIES

Afghanistan	National Assembly
Algeria	Parliament
Australia	Parliament of Australia
Austria	Federal Assembly
Bangladesh	Jatiya Sangsad
Belgium	Federal Parliament
Bhutan	Parliament of Bhutan
Brazil	National Assembly and Senate Parliament
Britain	Parliament House of Commons and House of Lords
Cambodia	National Assembly
Canada	Parliament (House of Commons and Senate)
China	National People's Cogress
Denmark	Folketing
Egypt	Parliament
France	Parliament
Germany	Bundestag (Lower House) and Bundesrat (Upper House)
Holland	States General
Hungary	National Assembly
Iceland	Althing
India	Sansad (Lok Sabha and Rajya Sabha)

Indonesia	People's Consultative Assembly
Ireland	Oireachtas
Israel	Knesset
Iran	Majlis
Iraq	Council of Representatives of Irag
Japan	Diet
Malaysia	Parlimen
Maldives	Majlis
Mongolia	State Great Hural
Myanmar	Pyidaungsu Hluttaw
Norway	Storting
Poland	National Assembly (Zgromadzenie Narodowe)
Romania	Parlementul
Saudi Arabia	Majlis Al-Shura
Spain	Cortes Generales
Sudan	National Legislature Majlis Watani
Sweden	Riksdag
Switzerland	Federal Assembly
Syria	People's Assembly (Mailisal-Sha'ab)
Tanzania	Bunge
USA	Congress (House of Representatives and Senate)

FAMOUS BORDER LINES

Radcliff Line

- It is a boundary line between Pakistan and Afghanistan.

Durand Line

- It is a boundary line between India and Pakistan.

Hindenborg Line

- It defines the boundary between Germany and Poland.

Maginot Line

- It is the boundary line between France and Germany.

McMahon Line

- It is a boundary line between India and Tibet (China), fixed in a conference held at Shimla in 1914.

Siegfried Line

- It is a line of fortifications drawn by Germany on her borders with France.

17th Parallel

- It defines the boundary between North Vietnam and South Vietnam before the two were united.

38th Parallel

- It is a boundary line between North Korea and South Korea.

49th Parallel

- It is the boundary line between the USA and Canada.

4

GEOGRAPHY OF THE WORLD

Land and Water

- Our earth has a total surface area of about 52 crore sq km.
- Land occupies about 29 percent and water 71 percent of the globe. In the Northern Hemisphere; land and water areas are almost equal; but in Southern Hemisphere, water is about 15 times as much as land.

Continents of the World

- There are seven continents in the world: Asia, Africa, Europe, North America, South America, Australia and Antarctica.
- The total surface area is 510,056,570 sq km.
- Asia – 43,999,000 sq km.
- Africa – 29,800,000 sq km.
- North America – 24,320,000 sq km.
- South America – 17,599,000 sq km.
- Europe – 9,700,000 sq km.
- Australia – 7,682,300 sq km.
- Antarctica – 14,000,000 sq km.

Asia

- The largest continent, it extends over nearly one-third of the land surface of earth.
- Mountain Peaks: Himalayas, Kunlun, Tie Shah, Altai and Tibetan Plateau.
- Rivers: Brahmaputra, Ganga, Yang-tze Kiang, Yamuna, Yenisei, Amur, Hwang-ho and Mekong.
- Climate: Varied, extreme in north, monsoonal in south and east.
- Minerals: Gold, coal, iron, manganese, etc.

Africa

- It is the second largest continent.
- It is bounded on the north by the Mediterranean Sea, in the east by the Red Sea and the Indian Ocean, and in the west by the Atlantic Ocean.
- It is roughly triangular in shape.
- The highest mountain of this continent is Kilimanjaro.
- Rivers: Nile, Congo (Zaire), Niger, Zambebi. The largest lake is Victoria.
- Minerals: Gold, diamond and copper.
- Products: Cocoa, palm oil, groundnut, coffee, cotton, wheat, maize and wool.
- Cities: Cairo, Lusaka, Cape Town, Mombasa, Nairobi, Adis Ababa, Salisbury, Pretoria.

Europe

- In area, it is larger than Australia and smaller than other continents.
- Mountains: Alps, Pyrannes, Apennines, Urals and Caucasus.

- Rivers: Volga, Danube, Rhine, Don, Ural.
- Lakes: Ladoga, Onega, Peipus and Viatern.
- Minerals: Petroleum, iron and coal.
- Products: Paper, fish, dairy products, sugar beet, potatoes, fruits, wheat, rice, maize.

North America

- It comprises Mexico, USA, Canada, Greenland, Central American States and the West Indies.
- Climate: Temperate and tropical.
- Products: Cereals, tobacco, sugar beet, potatoes, etc.
- Minerals: Coal, petroleum, iron, manganese, etc.
- General Industry: Ship-building.

South America

- Its climate is diverse, varying with latitude and altitude, equatorial, hot and wet. Atacama, a rainless desert in the middle west coast in the south, is temperate.
- Industries: Tropical agriculture: cocoa, coffee, sugarcane, rubber cereals, etc.
- Minerals: Gold, silver, copper, tin, diamond and nitrates. Factories and industries are developing gradually.

Australia

- Australia is an island continent. It comprises the following states: New South Wales (*Cap.* Sydney), Queensland (*Cap.* Brisbane), South Australia (*Cap.* Adelaide), Western Australia (*Cap.* Perth), Victoria (*Cap.* Melbourne), Tasmania (*Cap.* Hobart). All capital cities are ports, though Perth is served by the port of Fremantle.

- An area largely uninhabited in the Northern Territory. Its capital is Darwin. The territory does not yet govern itself in the way other states do. The federal capital is Canberra.
- Australia produces more wool than any other country in the world. The country also has rich supplies of gold, iron ore, lead and zinc and has a new growing steel industry.
- One of the most important rivers is the Snowy in New South Wales and Victoria.

THE EARTH

Shape of Earth

- Earth appears to be flat but, in reality, it is oblate spheroid.
- It is a little flattened at the poles and bulges out a little at the Equator.
- Earth related facts

  Mass of Earth: 6.58×10^{21} tons (approx.)

  Density of Earth: 5.517 times that of water.

  Volume of Earth: 1,083, 208, 840, 000 cu. km.

  Equatorial Circumference: 40,076 km.

  Polar Circumference: 40,007.89 km.

  Equatorial Diameter: 12,755 km.

  Polar Diameter: 12,712 km.
- The age of earth is estimated to be around 5,000 million years.

The Crust of Earth

- This hard and solid outer portion of the earth is called its crust or *Lithosphere.*

- It is about 50 km thick.
- The crust of earth consists of the following elements:

  Oxygen 49.85%

  Silicon 26.03%

  Aluminium 7.28%

  Iron 4.12%

  Calcium 3.18%

  Soda 2.33%

The Surface of Earth (Biosphere)

The Surface of earth is conveniently divided into four spheres:

- **Lithosphere:** The solid crust consist of soil and hard rock which is relatively thin and in which different land forms are found.
- **Hydrosphere:** All the water of earth, including the oceans, lakes, rivers, ice-sheets and the water in the atmosphere.
- **Atmosphere:** The envelop of air that surrounds the earth.
- **Magnetosphere:** The space surrounding the earth in which there is a magnetic field associated with that body.

Composition of the Atmosphere

- Pure air consists of Nitrogen 78.03%, Oxygen 20.99%, Carbon dioxide 0.03%, Inert gas 0.95% by volume. Water vapours and dust impurities are found in traces.
- Earth's axis is inclined on earth's plane by 66½° on the plane of the orbit. This axis always points in the same direction.

Earth's Axis

- The earth rotates round on its axis from west to east once in twenty-four hours. This motion of the earth is called rotation.
- The rotation of the earth is the real cause of the apparent rising and setting of the sun which, in fact, is stationary. Its effects are:
    - Days and nights are formed.
    - The sun, the moon and the stars appear to revolve around the earth.
    - Winds and currents change their direction.
    - Different places have different local times.
    - Tides occur regularly, twice a day.
- The speed of earth's rotation at the equator is about 1,666 km per hour.
- The speed becomes gradually slower towards the poles where it becomes zero.
- The average speed is 28 km per minute.

Revolution

- The earth revolves round the sun once in approximately 365¼ days, i.e. the period we call a year.
- This motion of the earth around the sun is called revolution.
- The earth revolves in a fixed path at a speed of 1,06,560 km per hour. This path is called the orbit. Its effects are:
    - This motion of the earth brings about changes in seasons.

- Days and nights are of unequal lengths at the same place at different times.
- Orbit of the earth is the elliptical path around the sun.

Related Terms

- **Perihelion:** The position of the earth or any planet when it is nearest to the sun. The earth reaches its perihelion in the beginning of January.
- **Aphelion:** The point on the earth or any other planet's orbit when it is farthest from the sun. Earth reaches its aphelion at the end of June.
- **Equinoxes:** March 21 and September 23, when days and nights are of equal duration throughout the globe, are called equinoxes.
- **Equality of Days and Nights:** At the Equator, days and nights are equal throughout the year because the circle of illumination always divides the equator into two equal parts.
- **Temperature Zones:** Ancient Greeks divided the globe into five main regions according to temperature. These regions are called Zones.
- **Torrid Zone:** It lies between 23½° North and $2^{3}/_{2}$° South, that is, between the Tropic of Cancer and the Tropic of Capricorn. The rays of sun are more nearly perpendicular here than in any other zone.
- **North Temperate Zone:** It lies between 23½° North (Tropic of Cancer) and 66½° North (Arctic Circle).
- **South Temperate Zone:** It lies between 23½°. South (Tropic of Capricorn) and 66½° South (Antarctic Circle).

- **South Frigid Zone:** It lies between 66½° South and 90° South, that is around South Pole. It, too, is extremely cold throughout the year.

International Date Line

- Ships crossing this line from west to east, (i.e. from China to the US) repeat a day. That is, if they cross it on Monday, December 10, the next day will also be counted as Monday, December 10.
- On the other hand, ships crossing this line from east to west, (i.e. from the US to China) drop a day, that is, if they cross it on Monday, December 10, the next day will be counted as Wednesday, December 12.
- The International Date Line normally corresponds to 180° meridian, however, does not everywhere coincide with 180° meridian; at places deviates a little from it. The reason for this is that 180° meridian passes through some group of islands, called Aluteian Trench and Kurli Trench, belonging to the same government.
- **Meridian:** Meridians are imaginary lines (half circles) which join the two poles.
- **Prime Meridian:** It is the Meridian from which longitude is measured. It is numbered 0° longitude. It is the meridian which passes through Greenwich (near London) where there was once a famous observatory.
- **Latitude:** It is distance of a place north or south of equator along a meridian. This distance is measured in degrees.
- **Longitude:** It is the distance of a place east or west

of the Prime Meridian along a parallel of latitude. Note: The difference in time per degree logitude between any two places on the globe is 4 minutes.

ROCKS

Igneous Rocks

- There are two main classes of igneous rocks: First, that are formed by the cooling of the hot, molten matter on the surface of the earth are called Volcanic Rocks and the second, that are formed by the cooling of the hot molten matter deep within the earth are called Plutonic Rocks.
- The most important example of the first kind is basalt and that of the second kind is granite, which is harder and more durable than basalt.
- Igneous rocks are also called Primary Rocks because they were the first to be formed when the outer layers of the molten earth solidified.
- These rocks now appear on the earth's surface over small areas, e.g. Brazil, Tableland of Africa, Western Australia, North-East Canada and Deccan.
- The black soil of Deccan, also called the *Deccan Trap,* consists of basalt rocks.

Sedimentary Rocks

- They contain most of the minerals of the world.
- The important sedimentary rocks are clay, limestone, sandstone, chalk and coal.
- The chief characteristic of sedimentary rocks is that they are found in layers. So, they are also called stratified rocks.

There are two kinds of sedimentary rocks:

- *Rocks* formed by the deposition of materials derived from land: Conglomerate, sandstone, shale (mudstone) were formed in this way. These rocks are called Inorganic Rocks: The Ganga plain consists of sedimentary rocks.
- Rocks formed by the deposition of plants and sea organisms are called Organic Rocks and the internal heat changed them into *coal.*

Metamorphic Rocks

- Metamorphic rocks are those rocks which were formerly igneous or sedimentary rocks that changed owing to extreme heat and pressure of the earth.
- Slate, which in reality is shale and marble, which in reality is limestone, are example of metamorphic rocks.
- Other examples of metamorphic rocks are quartzite (originally sandstone) and graphite (originally coal).
- Most of the Deccan Plateau consists of Metamorphic Rocks.

MOUNTAINS

Fold Mountains

- Fold mountains are those mountains which were formed as a result of a part of earth's surface being thrown up into folds or wrinkles by the movement of the earth's crust.
- The great mountains of the world like the Himalayas, Alps, Rockies and Andes are fold mountains.

Block Mountains

- Block mountains are those mountains which were

formed by the rising up of a block of the earth's surface between two cracks or faults.

- Vosges mountains of France, Black Forest of Germany, the *Siera* Navada in the US, Pennines in England and the mountains of Spain among other are block mountains.

Residual Mountains

- Residual mountains are remnants of old mountains and plateaus which have been left over after their comparatively soft parts have been worn away by wind and weather. Nilgiri Hills and Rajmahal Hills are examples of residual mountains.

Volcanic Mountains

- Volcanic mountains are those conical mountains which have been formed by the accumulation of lava.
- Fujiyama of Japan and Vesuvius of Italy etc are examples of volcanic mountains.
- On account of great heat, the rocks deep down below the earth's surface are hot and molten. These molten rocks are called magma.
- Sometimes, because of great pressure, magma forces its way through some part of weak crust to the earth's surface. It is then called lava.

OCEANS

- Oceans cover about 70.8 percent of the surface of the earth.
- The average depth of the oceans is nearly 3.5 kilometres and their salinity is 3.5%.

- All the water on earth's surface is called hydrosphere. Of this, 97.3% of total water is in the oceans and inland seas.
- The remaining 2.7% is found as glaciers and ice caps, fresh water lakes, rivers and underground water.
- **Pacific Ocean:** The largest (area about 166,240,000 sq km) and the deepest ocean. It is bounded by North America and South America on the east and Australia and Asia on the west. Covers more than one-third of the surface of the earth and is bigger than the combined area of all the continents.
- **Atlantic Ocean:** The second biggest ocean. To its east lie Europe and Africa, to its west is America. Atlantic Ocean is the world's saltiest ocean. Its area is about 86,560,000 sq km.
- **Indian Ocean:** To its north lies Asia, to its west Africa and to its east are East Indies (Indonesia) and Australia. This is the only ocean named after a country. Its area is about 4,430,000 sq km.
- **Arctic Ocean:** Surrounds the North Pole and lies to the north of Asia, Europe and North America. On account of intense cold, it remains frozen almost the whole of the year. Its area is about 22,280,000 sq km.
- **Antarctic Ocean:** Lies near the South Pole. Its upper surface also remains frozen for the greater part of the year. Antarctic Ocean is also called the Southern Ocean. Antarctic ocean is now being explored by a number of nations. India has also set up two permanent research stations, namely, Dakshin Gangotri and Maitrayi. Its area is about 22,280,000 sq km.

EFFECTS OF OCEAN CURRENTS ON CLIMATE

Variation in Temperature

- The meeting of cold and warm currents causes variation in temperature. This, in turn, causes heavy storms, e.g. Hurricanes are frequent near Newfoundland.
- Warm currents raise and cold currents lower the temperature of the coastal regions along which they flow. For instance; Labrador and the British Isles are nearly in the same latitude but Labrador coast remains ice bound for about nine months in the year on account of the cold Labrador Current, while the climate of Great Britain is comparatively mild on account of the Gulf Stream.

Variation in Rainfall

- Countries influenced by warm currents receive more rainfall than countries influenced by cold currents. Western Europe receives heavy rainfall on account of the Gulf Stream while the west coast of South Africa is dry on account of the cold Benguela Current.

State of Fogs

- Dense fogs are produced where warm and moist air over the warm currents come in contact with the cold air over the cold currents. Fog is produced near Newfoundland on account of the cold Labrador Current joining the warm Gulf Stream.

Economic Importance of Currents

- Open Harbours: The harbours of cold countries which are under the influence of warm currents remain open all the year round. The harbours of Great Britain and Norway remain open all the year round on account of the warm Gulf Stream.

- Influence on Fish Trade: The best fish is found in cold, shallow water. But cold currents flowing to warmer regions carry fish also along with them. Thus, (fish is available) in warm latitudes too.
- Sea water remains pure: On account of ocean currents, sea water remains in motion and hence keeps pure.
- Influence on navigation: Currents help or hinder navigation. Ships (especially sailing ships) sailing along a current pick up greater speed while ships sailing against a current get slowed down.

LAYERS OF ATMOSPHERE

Troposphere

- It is the lowest thick layer of atmosphere extending to an average altitude of 10 km above the earth's surface.
- The temperature in this layer decreases by 1°C for every 165 metres or 500 ft.
- This layer contains dust particles, water vapours and clouds. Most of the weather changes take place in this sphere.

Stratosphere

- It extends up to about 50 km above the earth's surface. Its rich layer of ozone absorbs most of the harmful ultraviolet radiation and thereby protects life. It provides ideal conditions for flying large aeroplanes. The temperature in this layer remains almost constant.

Mesosphere

- It is a very cold region above the ozone-rich layer of stratosphere. It extends to a height of 80 km above the earth.

Ionosphere

- It extends from 80 to 1,000 km above the earth.
- This region contains ionised or electrically charged air and reflects radio waves facilitating wireless communications between different places.
- The ionised air also protects those on earth from falling materials, most of which are made to burn out in this region.

Thermosphere

- The region beyond ionosphere is called thermosphere. The heated-up layers of the uppermost atmosphere have very high temperature.

Exosphere

- It is the upper-most region of atmosphere where the air density is lower than an air molecule, moving rapidly straight forward, and is more than 50 percent likely to escape from atmosphere instead of hitting other molecules.

WEATHER AND CLIMATE

Weather

- Weather means the condition of the atmosphere of a place with respect to temperature, rainfall, winds, humidity, sunshine and cloudiness existing at any given time.

Climate

- Climate means the average weather conditions of a place or area with respect to temperature, rainfall, winds, humidity, etc., over a number of years.
- To know the weather, the condition of the atmosphere is observed for a very short period, e.g. a day, two days or a week; but climate is the average condition of the weather of that place for a considerable period, say, 30 or 35 years.

Kinds of Winds

- Constant or Permanent Winds: These winds always blow in the same direction. The Trade Winds and Anti-Trade Winds (Westerlies) are such wind. They are also called Planetary Winds.
- Periodic Winds: These winds blow in one direction at a particular time or during a particular season and in the opposite direction at another time or season. The Monsoons and the Land and Sea Breezes are periodic wind.
- Variable Winds: These winds are irregular winds, as the Cyclones and Anti-cyclones.

Trade Winds

- Trade winds are constant winds, which blow towards the equator. Generally, these winds blow from 30°N and 30°S towards the equator, i.e., they blow in tropical latitudes. In the northern hemisphere, their direction is north-east and in the southern hemisphere, south-east.

Change of the Wind Direction

- Trade Winds blow from north to south in the northern hemisphere and south to north in the southern hemisphere.

Anti-Trade Winds

- Westerlies or Anti-Trade Winds are constant winds which blow from 30°N to 60°S, i.e. over temperate latitudes.
- In the northern hemisphere, their direction is south-west and in the southern hemisphere north-west.
- These winds are called Westerlies because in both the hemispheres, they appear to blow from the west.

Monsoons

- Monsoons are periodical winds which blow from sea to land for six months in summer and from land to sea for six months in winter.
- They occur where there is a large landmass near sea within the tropics or near the tropics.
- They are caused by the unequal heating of land and sea in summer and winter.
- They blow over South-East Asia, East Asia, Australia, New Zealand and Malagasy (Madagascar).

Summer Monsoons

- The air above the Indian Ocean and the Pacific Ocean is comparatively cold and heavy and has high pressure. Therefore, winds from the Indian Ocean and the South-West Pacific Ocean blow towards these plains.
- Since they come from the sea, they bring heavy rains.

Winter Monsoons

- Winds blowing from the south are South-East monsoons. When they cross the equator, they turn to their left and become north-west winds. In Australia, they are known as North-West monsoons. These winds blow from November to April.

Effect of Monsoons

- In India, 90% of the total rainfall is from these summer monsoons and the prosperity of India depends on these winds.
- Winter monsoons, being land winds, bring no rains. But as they blow over the Bay of Bengal, they pick up some moisture and when they strike against the Eastern Ghats and the mountains of Sri Lanka, they bring rain to Tamil Nadu and the east coast of Sri Lanka.
- The paddy crop of Tamil Nadu during these months depends on these winds. These winds bring rain to Australia also.

Cyclones

- On account of rotation of the earth, these winds assume a circular form. A large low pressure region, in which the winds blow spirally towards a central region of low pressure, is called cyclone.

Anti-Cyclones

- The large high pressure region in which the winds blow spirally outwards from a central region of high pressure is called an anti-cyclone.

Form of Condensation : Fog

- When hot, moist air comes into contact with cold air or cold water, it is cooled and some of the water vapours condense around the floating particles of dust in the atmosphere. This is called fog. The presence of dust particles in the air is necessary for the formation of fog.

Mist

- Mist and fog are identical terms. These are formed in the same way, the only difference being that in fog, the particles of water are smaller and the visibility is poorer than in the mist.
- Clouds are formed in the upper regions of the atmosphere. Dust particles are necessary for the formation of clouds.

Hail

- When raindrops on their way to the earth are carried upwards by air currents into colder regions, they freeze and become hail.

Snow

- When the clouds ascend to intensely cold regions of the atmosphere, they freeze without passing through the liquid form and fall as snow.

Dew

- When vapour-laden (moist) air touches the grass, flowers and leaves, it becomes cool and cannot hold all the water vapours. Some of these water vapours are condensed and they settle down on their surfaces in the form of water drops which is called dew.

Frost

- Frost is frozen dew. In very cold countries, the temperature of surface of the earth at night falls even below freezing and becomes frost. This frost causes great harm to the crops.
- Dew and frost are formed on the surface of the earth.
- Mist and fog are formed near the surface of the earth.

- Cloud, rain and snow are formed at a considerable height above the surface of the earth.

Rainfall

There are three necessary conditions for the formation of rain:

- Evaporation.
- Condensation.
- Presence of dust particles in the air.

Rain Shadow

- The side of the mountain where the moisture-laden winds strike and bring rain is called the windward side; while the other side; which is comparatively dry, is called the leeward side.
- The rainless area on the leeward side of mountains is called the rain shadow.

GAZETTEER : A GEOGRAPHICAL INDEX OF THE WORLD

- Abadan (Iran): Noted for oil refinery.
- Alexandria (Egypt): Founded by Alexander; handles about 80 percent of the export of Egypt.
- Amarkantak: It is the source of peninsular river Narmada and Tapti in Madhya Pradesh.
- Antarctica: It is the frozen continent covering 14 million sq km around South Pole.
- Bavel Mandeb Mandal: It is a strait connecting Red Sea and Indian Ocean.
- Baku (Azerbaijan): On Caspian Sea; noted for petroleum.

- Bali Island (Indonesia): Famous for Hindu monuments and temples.
- Bolan Pass: A pass in the mountains of north-east Baluchistan (Pakistan) from lower Indus to Kandhar; now traversed by a railway.
- Bosphorus: It is strait between Black Sea and Sea of Marmara.
- Chicago (USA): It is situated on Lake Michigan and is the greatest grain and meat market in the world.
- Colombo (Sri Lanka): Capital and chief port; coaling station and of much strategic value.
- Coolgarline: A gold mining town in West Australia.
- Cotopaxi: It is an active volcano in the Andes mountains of South America.
- Cuba: A West Indies island famous for cigars and tobacco.
- Dakshin Gangotri: It is first permanent manned station established by India in Antarctica.
- Dead Sea: It is a salt-water lake between Israel and Jordan. Its surface is 1,286 feet below the level of the Mediterranean.
- Detroit (USA): Famous for the manufacture of motor cars.
- Diego Garcia: It is a very tiny island in the Indian Ocean located to the south of Sri Lanka. It is in possession of Britain. Here the USA had constructed a naval and air base as part of its strategy to counter Soviet influence in the Indian Ocean.

- Dundee (UK): City and seaport of Great Britain; centre of jute and linen manufacture.
- Durban (South Africa): Largest diamond trading centre in the world.
- Elba: Island of Mediterranean Sea; belongs to Italy. Napoleon had lived here in exile from May 1814 to February 1815.
- Mt. Etna (Italy): It is the name of a great volcanic mountain.
- Mt. Everest (Nepal): Highest peak of the world in the Himalayas (8,848 metres).
- Geneva (Switzerland): Headquarters of International Red Cross Society.
- Golan heights: It is a mountainous region in Syria where the boundaries of the country touch that of Israel.
- Greenwich (England): Famous for its observatory from which standard time is reckoned. First Meridian begins from here.
- Hague (Netherlands): Headquarters of International Court of Justice.
- Havana (Cuba): Capital; noted for cigars. Columbus was buried here.
- Hawaii (USA): Island in the centre of Pacific, well-known for its beechs and as an essential point on America-Japan trade route.
- Hiroshima (Japan): Sea Port; First city to be destroyed by atomic bomb on August 6, 1945.
- Hollywood (USA): Chief centre of film industry in the world.

- Hong Kong: It is a free exchange port; transferred to China in 1997.
- Java (Indonesia): Biggest island of Indonesia; famous for rubber and sugar.
- Jerusalem (Israel): Holy city for three world faiths – Muslims, Jews and Christians.
- Johannesburg (South Africa): Famous for gold mines.
- Kahuta (Pakistan): Famous for nuclear research centre.
- Kanchenjunga: It is India's highest and world's third highest peak (height 8,598 metres). It stands in the Himalayas on the border between Napal and Sikkim.
- Kimberley (South Africa): Centre of diamond mines.
- Lumbini (Nepal): Birthplace of Lord Buddha.
- Maastricht (Netherlands): Famous historical city.
- Mahadeo Hills: Famous hills in Madhya Pradesh.
- Maitri: It is the second permanent station established by India in Antarctica.
- Marseilles (France): Halting place on Suez route to Europe.
- Mecca (Saudi Arabia): Place of birth of Prophet Mohammad; place of pilgrimage for Muslims.
- Messina: It is a strait between Sicily and Italian mainland.
- Mont Blanc: It is the highest mountain in Europe. It is in the Alps on the confines of Italy and France.

- Mururua Atoll (French Polynesia): Noted for French nuclear tests.
- Nagasaki (Japan): The city where the atom bomb was dropped by USA on August 9, 1945.
- Nuremburg (Germany): Here the famous trial of Nazi war criminals was held.
- Pamirs: It is the highest plateau of the world which is situated at the north-west area of Tibet. Pamir is called the roof of the world.
- Pearl Harbour (USA): It is a naval base on the Hawaiian island. The Japanese attacked it on December 7, 1941.
- Pittsburgh (USA): Biggest iron and steel centre in the world.
- Rajkamal Hills: These are mountains in Madhya Pradesh from which Mahanadi river originates.
- Red Sea: Arm of the sea joining the Arabian Sea with the Mediterranean Sea through Suez Canal route to the east. Of high strategic importance.
- Ruhr: River of Germany. Flows through a great industrial district of the same name which has many iron and steel manufacturing centres.
- Siachen: It is the name of a glacier north of the Nubra Valley in Jammu & Kashmir.
- Stratford-upon-Avon (England): Birth place of Shakespeare.
- Sunderbans: Part of gangetic delta; jungle area famous for mangroves and tigers.

- Taxila (Pakistan): Famous for the excavations by Sir John Marshal. Old seat of Buddhist University.
- United Arab Republic: It is the union of seven emirates in Parsian Gulf. These are Abu Dhabi, Dubai, Sharjah, Umm-al-quiwin, Ajman, Fujairah and Ras-al-Khaimah.
- Verkhoyansk (CIS): The coldest place in the world.
- Yellowstone National Park (USA): A national American reserve established and maintained on a broad plateau in the rocky mountains.

Cities Situated on Riversides

City	Country	River
Alexandria	Egypt	Nile
Amsterdam	Netherlands	Amsel
Antwerp	Belgium	Scheldt
Bangkok	Thailand	Menam
Belgrade	Yugoslavia	Danube
Berlin	Germany	Spree
Bonn	Germany	Rhine
Budapest	Hungary	Danube
Buenos Aires	Argentina	Plate
Bucharest	Romania	Dimbovitya
Cairo	Egypt	Nile
Delhi	India	Yamuna
Dublin	Ireland	Liffy

City	Country	River
Glasgow	Scotland	Clyde
Guwahati	India	Brahmaputra
Hamburg	Germany	Elbe
Kanpur	India	Ganga
Kinshasa	Zaire	Congo
Lahore	Pakistan	Ravi
Leningrad	Russia	Neva
Lisbon	Portugal	Tagus
Liverpool	England	Mersey
London	England	Thames
Mandalay	Myanmar	Irrawady
Montreal	Canada	St. Lawrence
Moscow	Russia	Muskva
New York	USA	Hudson
Ottawa	Canada	Ottawa
Paris	France	Seine
Philadelphia	USA	Delaware
Prague	Czech Republic	Vilava
Quebec	Canada	St. Lawrence
Rome	Italy	Tiber
Shanghai	China	Yang-Tse-Kiang
Tokyo	Japan	Sumida
Varanasi	India	Ganga
Vienna	Austria	Danube

City	Country	River
Warsaw	Poland	Vistula
Washington	USA	Potomac
Yangon	Myanmar	Irrawady

Mineral Producers in the world

Mineral	*Largest*	*2nd Largest*	*3rd Largest*
Coal	China	USA	Australia
Iron Ore	China	Brazil	Australia
Aluminium	China	Russia	Canada
Gold	South Africa	China	Australia
Silver	Mexico	Peru	China
Manganese	China	South Africa	Australia
Mica	India	-	-
Petroleum	Russia	Saudi Arabia	United States

Largest Producers of the World

Articles	Producers	Articles	Producers
Carpets	Iran	Cheese	USA
Coffee	Brazil	Copper	Chile
Cotton	China	Diamonds	Botswana
Jute	Bangladesh	Rice	China
Rubber	Thailand	Silk	China
Steel	China	Sugar	India
Tea	India	Tin	China
Wheat	China	Wool	Australia

Largest Countries and their Areas

Rank		Area (sq km)
1.	Russia	17,075,200
2.	Canada	9,976,140
3.	United States	9,629,091
4.	China	9,596,960
5.	Brazil	8,511,965
6.	Australia	7,686,850
7.	India	3,287,590
8.	Argentina	2,776,890
9.	Sudan	2,505,810
10.	Algeria	2,381,741

Largest Islands in the World

Name	Location	Area in (sq km)
1. Greenland	North Atlantic	2,175,597
2. New Guinea	South-West Pacific	820,003
3. Borneo	West-mid-Pacific	743,107
4. Madagascar	Indian Ocean	587,042
5. Baffin	North Atlantic	476,068

Principle Rivers in the World

River	Outflow	Length (km)
1. Nile	Mediterranean Sea	6,690
2. Amazon	Atlantic Ocean	6,296
3. Mississippi Missouri	Gulf of Mexico	6,240

4. Yangtze Kiang	China Sea	5,797
5. Amur-Argun	Tatar Strait	5,780

Highest Mountains in the World

Mountain Peak	**Range**	**Height (m)**
1. Mount Everest	Himalayas	8,848
2. K-2 (Godwin Austen)	Karakoram	8,611
3. Kanchenjunga	Himalayas	8,598
4. Lhotse	Himalayas	8,511
5. Makalu I	Himalayas	8,481
6. Dhaulagiri I	Himalayas	8,172
7. Manaslu I	Himalayas	8,156
8. Cho Uyo	Himalayas	8,153
9. Nanga Parbat	Himalayas	8,126
10. Annapurna I	Himalayas	8,078

Highest Waterfalls in the World

Name	**Location**	**Height (Mtrs.)**
1. Angel	Venezuela	1,000
2. Tugela	South Africa	914
3. Cuquenan	Venezuela	610
4. Sutherland	New Zealand	580
5. Takkakaw	British Columbia	503
6. Ribbon (Yosemite)	California	491
7. Upper Yosemite	California	436
8. Gavarnie	France	422
9. Vettisfoss	Norway	366
10. Widow's Tears	California	357

Largest Deserts in the World

Desert	Continent	Area (sq km)
1. Sahara	Africa	90,65,000
2. Australian Desert	Australia	1,550,000
3. Arabian Desert	Asia	1,300,000
4. Gobi	Asia	1,295,000
5. Kalahari Desert	Africa	520,000
6. Takla Makan	Asia	320,000
7. Sonoran Desert	North America	310,000
8. Namib Desert	Africa	310,000
9. Kara Kum	Asia	270,000
10. Thar	Asia (India)	260,000

5

GEOGRAPHY OF INDIA

Natural Regions, Rainfall, Soils and Forests

- India lies between latitudes 8°N and 37° North and longitudes 68°E and 97° East.
- The Tropic of Cancer passes right through the centre, cutting the country roughly into two parts, along Gujarat, Madhya Pradesh, Jharkhand, West Bengal, Tripura and Mizoram.

Area

- The area of the Indian Union is 32,87,263 sq km.
- It measures about 3,214 km from North to South and about 2,933 km from East to West.
- It has land frontier of 15,200 km and a coast line about 6,080 km (7,516 km including that of Lakshadweep and Andaman & Nicobar group of Islands).
- It has 2.4 percent of earth's surface area; it is the *seventh* largest country in the world.

Boundaries

- It is bounded on the north by China, Nepal and Bhutan; on the East by Myanmar and Bangladesh;

on the South by the Indian Ocean; and on the North West by Pakistan and Afghanistan.

Natural Regions

Himalayas and their Eastern Off-shoots

- It extends from Kashmir to Arunachal Pradesh over a distance of about 2,400 km.
- The highest peaks in the world are found in these ranges.
- Mount Everest is the highest peak of the world.
- The Himalayas provide rain for the plains by stopping moisture-bearing winds.

The Indo-Gangetic Plain

- This plain lies between Himalayas and Deccan Plateau from West Bengal to Punjab extending for about 2,400 km.
- The plain has two great river-valley systems – Ganges and its tributaries, and Indus and its tributaries.
- In this region, rainfall is heavy and agriculture is the main occupation of the people.
- Soil is very fertile and the climate is healthy.

The Deccan Plateau

- It lies to the south of Indo-Gangetic plain.
- On its north are Vindhyas (oldest mountain) and Satpura Hills, while Eastern and Western Ghats (Sahyadari) form its eastern and western boundaries, respectively.
- Both the Eastern and Western Ghats meet in the Nilgiri Hills.

- To the South of the Nilgiri Hills is the well-known Palghat Pass.
- There begin the Cardamom Hills of Kerala which extend as far as Kanyakumari.
- It has an average height of 600 metres above sea level.

Coastal Plains

- Coastal plains stretch along the western and eastern coasts of India.
- They are called the Western and Eastern (Coromandel) coastal plains.

Western Coastal Plains

- This coastal plain lies between Arabian Sea and the Western Ghats.
- Its northern plain is called Konkan and the southern part, Malabar.
- This plain is quite narrow and not more than 64 km broad.
- The plain is very fertile and gets heavy rainfall of about 200 cm annually.

Eastern Coastal Plains

- This plain lies between the Bay of Bengal and Eastern Ghats and is also called Coromandel.
- This plain is wider than Western Coastal Plain.
- It contains deltas of Mahanadi, Godavari, Krishna and Cauvery.

Rainfall

- This is a region of Heavy Rainfall. Here, minimum rainfall is 200 cm. This includes Meghalaya, Assam,

Arunachal Pradesh, Sikkim, northern parts of West Bengal, Western Coastal Plains, Western Ghats and the West Himalayan slopes.

- Region of Moderate Rainfall: Here rainfall is between 100 and 200 cm. It includes West Bengal, Bihar, Jharkhand, Eastern Uttar Pradesh, Uttarakhand, sub-mountain region of Punjab, Orissa, Madhya Pradesh, Chhattisgarh, East Coast of Tamil Nadu, Eastern slopes of Western Ghats.
- Region of Low Rainfall: Here rainfall is between 50 cm and 100 cm. It includes Deccan, Gujarat, Eastern Rajasthan, Western UP, Haryana and Northern Punjab.
- Region of Scanty Rainfall: Here rainfall is below 50 cm. It includes Kutch, Western Rajasthan, Southern Haryana, South-West Punjab, Central Deccan and Ladakh.

SOILS OF INDIA

Alluvial Soils

- The alluvial soils are generally confined to river basins and coastal plains.
- They contribute significantly to the development of agriculture in India.
- The alluvial soils vary from sandy loam to clay in texture.
- These are found in UP, Punjab, Haryana, Rajasthan, etc.

Black (Regur) Soils

- The black soils are concentrated over the Deccan Lava tract which includes parts of Maharashtra, Madhya Pradesh, Gujarat, Andhra Pradesh and some parts of Tamil Nadu.

- Chemically, the black soils consist of lime, iron, magnesia and alumina, and potash. But these lack phosphorus, nitrogen and organic matter.
- These are very useful for growing cotton.

Red Soils

- The soil develops a reddish colour due to presence of oxide of iron in ancient crystalline and metamorphic rocks.
- Red soil covers almost the whole of Tamil Nadu, Karnataka, Andhra Pradesh, South-eastern Maharashtra, eastern parts of Madhya Pradesh, parts of Odisha and Chota Nagpur and Bundelkhand – all of them lying on the periphery of the plateau.
- Red soil is comparatively porous and lacks nutrients, especially organic matter. As a result, this soil has limited fertility and is suitable for growing millets and rice.

Laterite Soils

- The formation of laterite soils takes place under typical monsoon conditions.
- The main development of these soils has taken place in the highland areas of the plateau.
- The laterite soils are commonly found in Karnataka, Kerala, Tamil Nadu and hilly areas of Odisha and Assam.

FORESTS OF INDIA

Dry Forests

- These forests are found in areas where annual rainfall is less than 100 cm.

- They are common in Rajasthan, Haryana, Kutch and dry areas of interior Deccan.

Deciduous Forests

- These trees shed their leaves once a year in hot weather.
- They are mostly found along the Himalayan foothills and on the north-eastern hilly areas of Deccan Plateau and the eastern slopes of Western Ghats.
- Their characteristic trees are sal, teak, sandalwood, rosewood and shisham.

Coniferous Forests

- These forests are found in areas of very heavy rainfall, i.e. over 200 cm.
- They are found mostly in West Bengal, Western Coastal Plains, the north-east hills and on the western slopes of Western Ghats.

Mountain Forests

- These forests are found on the slopes of the Himalayas but differ in kind with increasing height because climate gets colder.

Tidal Forests

- These are found in the deltas of rivers which are subject to tides.
- These forests yield tanning material and firewood.
- Their wood is also used for making boats and boxes.

Characteristics of forests

- The forests cover about 19.27 percent of the total geographical area of India.

- It is considered that a tropical country like India should have at least 33 percent of its area under forests to preserve proper climatic conditions.

INDIAN AGRICULTURE

- India is primarily an agricultural country and this sector of the economy accounts for nearly 23% of our national income.

Types of Cultivation

Sedentary Cultivation

- This is also known as settled cultivation.
- It is the practice of continued use of land year after year.

Shifting Cultivation

- In this practice land is cleared of forests and is used for a few years until the fertility of the soil decreases or the fields are taken over by weeds, etc.
- Then the cultivation is shifted to a new patch of land.

Terrace Cultivation

- Under this system, the mountain slopes are cut to form terraces and the land is used in the same manner as in sedentary cultivation.

Dry Cultivation

- This practice is followed in areas where facilities for irrigation are lacking. Crops grown in these areas can withstand dry conditions. Sometimes, the crops grown normally with irrigation are also grown under dry farming.

Intensive Cultivation

- This is the system under which small farms are used intensively with large inputs of manual labour, manures, fertilisers, etc.

Extensive Cultivation

- This type of farming is highly capital-intensive and is practised in sparsely populated areas.

Mixed and Multiple Farming

- The practice of growing more than one crop on the same land one after the other is called multiple farming or multiple cropping.

Crop Rotation

- A number of crops are grown one after the other in a fixed rotation to maintain the fertility of the soil. The rotation of crops may complete in a year in some of the areas while it may involve more than one year's time in others.

Fertility, Productivity and Agricultural Efficiency

- Fertility is the inherent capacity of land or soils to sustain plant growth. It is thus mainly a function of the nutrient content of the soil.
- Productivity is a measure of actual production of crops per unit of area. Productivity is measured in some standard terms or units.

CROPS

Kharif Crops

- These crops are sown at the beginning of the south-west monsoon season (May—July) and harvested at the end of this season (September—November).

- Major crops grown in this season include rice, jowar, bajra, maize, groundnut and jute.

Rabi Crops

- Sown at the beginning of the cold season (October–December) and harvested at the beginning of the warm season (February–April), these include wheat, gram, barley and potatoes.

Zaid Crops

- These crops are sown at the beginning of the season in February–March and August–September and are harvested in April–May and December–January. Summer vegetables, oil seeds and fodder crops like jowar are important among these crops.

MAJOR CROPS

Rice

- India is one of the major producers of rice in the world, accounting for nearly 20 percent of the total world production.
- Temperatures ranging between 20° and 30°C and receiving a well-distributed rainfall of about 100 cm or having irrigation facilities are suitable for growing rice.
- The most important areas producing rice in India are West Bengal, Andhra Pradesh, Tamil Nadu, Uttar Pradesh, Uttarakhand, Bihar, Jharkhand, Punjab and Assam. The states of Punjab and Haryana produce surplus of rice.
- Some important high-yielding varieties are Mansoori dwarf, Jaya, Padma Hamsa, Sabarmati and IET 1039 and 1136.

Wheat

- The ideal temperature for growing wheat is about 15°C to 20°C.
- It requires a moderate amount of rainfall or irrigation facilities.
- Loamy and clayey soils having good drainage are ideal for this crop.
- The major areas of wheat production in the country are Uttar Pradesh, Punjab, Haryana, Madhya Pradesh, Chhattisgarh and Rajasthan.
- Sonalika, Kalyan Sona and Sherbati are some of the high-yielding varieties of wheat.
- It is the crop which has lent the greatest support to the Green Revolution in Indian agriculture.

Maize

- The ideal temperature for growing maize is about 35°C and a precipitation of about 75 cm is required. The largest producer states are Uttar Pradesh, Rajasthan, Punjab, Bihar, Jharkhand, Chhattisgarh and Madhya Pradesh.

Bajra

- The amount of rainfall required for growing bajra is about 45 cm and the ideal temperature between 25° and 30°C.
- Most of the production of bajra comes from Gujarat, Rajasthan, Maharashtra and Haryana.

Jowar

- The crop of jowar requires a rainfall of 30 to 100 cm and temperature of 20° to 32°C.
- Green jowar serves as fodder for cattle and it is the

main use to which this crop is put in the north Indian plains.

- The major producers of jowar include Maharashtra, Madhya Pradesh, Karnataka and Andhra Pradesh.

Sugarcane

- India is the largest producer of sugarcane in the world. The country also has the distinction of having the largest area under this crop.
- The crop of sugarcane requires a rainfall of about 100 cm.
- The leading producers of sugarcane in India are Uttar Pradesh, Maharashtra, Bihar, Jharkhand, Tamil Nadu, Andhra Pradesh, Karnataka, Punjab and Haryana.

Cotton

- Cotton is one of the most important cash crops of India. It is a fibre crop and the cotton fibre is obtained from the fruit balls of the plant.
- The ideal geographical conditions for the cotton crop are : a precipitation of 50 to 80 cm and temperature of 20°C to 35°C.
- The ideal soil for this crop is black soil of the Deccan and Malwa plateaus, though alluvial and red soils can also be used.
- The most important producers of cotton are Gujarat, Maharashtra, Punjab, Karnataka, Haryana and Tamil Nadu.

Jute

- It is one of the cheapest and strongest fibres and makes for good packaging material.

- It is one of the highest foreign exchange earning crops of India.
- Jute grows best in areas of warm and humid climate having a temperature of 25°C to 35°C, receiving 100 to 200 cm rainfall.
- The chief producers of jute are West Bengal, Assam, Tripura, Odisha, Jharkhand and Bihar.

Tea

- The most suitable geographical conditions for cultivation of tea are: a heavy rainfall of more than 150 cm and a temperature of 24°C to 35°C.
- While the plant requires a lot of moisture, standing water is harmful for the roots of the plant. Due to this fact, tea is grown mainly on hill-slopes so that drainage is good.
- The most important areas of production are Assam, West Bengal and the Nilgiri Hills region.
- In India the tea from Darjeeling area of West Bengal is known for its flavour while the Assam tea is known for its strong taste.

Coffee

- Coffee is grown generally from 900 to 1,800 metres above sea level and larger trees like those of rubber are planted with coffee plants to provide shade.
- Karnataka, Kerala, Tamil Nadu and Andhra Pradesh are the leading coffee producers in India.

Rubber

- Natural rubber is obtained from latex (juice) of the tree which exudes naturally if a cut is made on its stem.
- The rubber tree requires a temperature of about 35°C

and more than 200 cm rainfall if a cut is made on its stem.

- Kerala produces about 90 percent India's natural rubber.

Tobacco

- Tobacco grows best in areas having a temperature of 15°C to 40°C and rainfall of over 50 cm or having irrigation facilities.
- The leading producer states in the country are Andhra Pradesh, Gujarat, Karnataka, Maharashtra, Bihar, Jharkhand, Tamil Nadu and Uttar Pradesh.
- Nicotina Tabacum and Nicotina Rustica are the most improtant varieties of tobacco grown in India.

Silk

- India is a traditional producer of silk. Out of many varieties of silk produced in India, mulberry and tasar are the most important.
- The major producers of silk in India are Karnataka, Jammu & Kashmir, Andhra Pradesh, Assam and Bihar. Bihar produces the largest amount of tasar silk.

RIVER SYSTEM AND MULTIPURPOSE RIVER VALLEY PROJECTS

- North India : Ganga, Yamuna, Ghagra, Gandak, Kosi, Sone, Chambal, Sutlej, Beas, Ravi and Brahmaputra.
- South India : Mahanadi, Godavari, Krishna and Cauvery flow into the Bay of Bengal; Narmada and Tapti flow into the Arabian Sea.
- Mahanadi originates from Rajkamal mountains of Madhya Pradesh.

- Narmada originates from Amarkantak of Madhya Pradesh. It flows between Vindhyas and Satpura.
- Tapti also originates from Amarkantak mountains of Madhya Pradesh.

Irrigation

- In India, about 40 percent of the total land area is under irrigation. Principal means of irrigation in India are:
- Canals: Punjab, Haryana, UP, Rajasthan, Tamil Nadu, Andhra Pradesh, Gujarat and Maharashtra.
- Wells: UP, Punjab and Haryana.
- Tanks: Andhra Pradesh, Karnataka and Tamil Nadu.
- Tube Wells: UP, Punjab, Haryana and Tamil Nadu.

Multipurpose River Valley Projects

Multipurpose projects are those which have got more than one object in view. Such as:

- Irrigation
- Flood control
- Generation of hydro-electric power
- Supply of drinking water
- Navigation
- Development of recreational spots
- Development of fisheries

The following projects provide these facilities to various Indian states:

Bhakra Nangal Project : Punjab, Haryana and Rajasthan

Bansagar Project: UP and Madhya Pradesh

Hirakund Project: Orissa

Tungabhadra Project : Andhra Pradesh and Karnataka

Farakka Dam : West Bengal

Nagarjuna Project: Andhra Pradesh

Poochampad Project: Andhra Pradesh

Gandak Project: Bihar, UP and Nepal

Kosi Project: Bihar

Ukai Multipurpose Project: Gujarat

Mahi Project: Gujarat

Upper Krishna Project: Karnataka

Ghataprabha Valley Project: Karnataka

Malaprabha Project: Karnataka

Tawa Project: Madhya Pradesh

Chambal Project: (MP) and Rajasthan

Bhima Project: Maharashtra

Jayakwadi Project: Maharashtra

Thein Project: Punjab

Indira Gandhi Canal: Rajasthan

Sarda Sahayak Project: UP

Ramganga Project: Uttarakhand

Kangsabati Project: West Bengal

Mayurakshi Project: West Bengal

Damodar Valley Project: West Bengal and Jharkhand

Sardar Sarovar Project: Gujarat, Maharashtra, Madhya Pradesh and Rajasthan

Tehri Dam Project: Uttarakhand

Salal Project: Jammu & Kashmir

Rihand Project: UP

Lower Sileru Project: UP

Sharavati Project: Karnataka

Sabarigiri Project: Kerala

Idukki Project: Kerala

Koyna Project: Maharashtra

Kundah Project: Tamil Nadu

Mahanadi Project: Orissa

Metatilla Project: UP

MINERALS

- More than 90 percent of the mineral deposits of the country are concentrated in the Chota Nagpur Plateau region.
- The only important mineral deposits outside this area are the petroleum deposits in Assam and Gujarat-Maharashtra region, the copper deposits of Rajasthan and the gold deposits of Karnataka.

Bauxite

- Bauxite is the ore used in the manufacture of aluminium.
- Important deposits of bauxite are located in Ranchi and Palamau districts of Jharkhand; Balaghat and Jabalpur districts of Madhya Pradesh; Bilaspur district of Chhattisgarh; and Belgaum and Thane Districts of Maharashtra.

Coal

- It occurs in the rocks of gondwana and tertiary formations. Large deposits of Gondwana formations occur in Jharia, Giridih and Bokaro in Jharkhand, Raniganj in West Bengal; Chanda and Panch Valley in Madhya Pradesh; Singareni in Andhra Pradesh.

Lignite

- This form of coal having 70% corbon content occurs in Gujarat, Tamil Nadu (Neyveli), Rajasthan (Palau) and Kashmir.
- Neyveli district in Tamil Nadu has the distinction of having the largest deposits of lignite in the country.

Copper

- The important deposits are located in Agnigundala in Andhra Pradesh; Singhbhum, Mosabani and Rakha in Jharkhand; Balaghat in Madhya Pradesh; Jhunjuna and Alwar in Rajasthan.

Diamond

- Diamond is a very pure form of carbon.
- In India, diamonds are mined only in Madhya Pradesh.
- Panna diamond belt is the most important area in this state for diamond mines.

Gold

- Presently, there are three important areas where gold is being mined, namely, the Ramagiri gold-field (Anantapur district) in Andhra Pradesh; Kolar gold-field in Kolar district of Karnataka; and the Hutti mines in Raichur district of Karnataka.

Graphite

- Graphite deposits of India are located in Orissa, Tamil Nadu, Andhra Pradesh, Jharkhand, Gujarat,

Karnataka, Kerala, Madhya Pradesh and Rajasthan. Odisha is the largest producer.

Gypsum

- Deposits of gypsum occur mainly in Jodhpur and Bikaner districts of Rajasthan and Kashmir, and in Tiruchirapalli district of Tamil Nadu.
- This mineral is used in the manufacture of cement and chemical fertilisers.

Iron ore

- Large deposits of iron occur in Singhbhum district in Jharkhand, Keonjar, Talcher and Mayurbhanj, in Odisha and Bailadilla in Madhya Pradesh.
- The quality of Indian iron deposits is good and there are many buyers for it in the world market.

Lead and Zinc

- These two minerals are generally found together.
- The known reserves of lead and zinc ore are located in Zawar and Banjavi areas in Rajasthan and Gujarat.
- Lead deposits are located in Agnigundala (Andhra Pradesh) and Sargipalle (Odisha).

Manganese

- India ranks fourth in the world in respect of manganese.
- This mineral is used as one of the raw materials in iron and steel industry.
- Good deposits of manganese are located in Madhya Pradesh, Chhattisgarh, Karnataka, Maharashtra, Orrisa, Andhra Pradesh and Tamil Nadu.

Marble

- Marble is used mainly as a building material and Indian marble stone is of very good quality.

- Large deposits of this rock are found in Rajasthan. Makrana is famous for the quality of marble stone found there.

Mica

- It is commonly used in electrical appliances as an insulating material.
- India is one of the *largest producers* of mica in the world.
- Jharkhand is the largest producer of mica in the country and here more than 75 percent of the production comes from Hazaribagh district.
- Kodarma mines in this region are the important mica-producing mines.

Natural Gas

- Natural gas is an important source of energy. It is found mainly along with petroleum deposits.
- The important gas reserves of India lie in Assam and Gujarat states.

Petroleum

- Important oil fields of India lie in Assam, Gujarat and in the off-shore area of Bombay High.
- In addition, oil deposits have been located in Godavari Basin and Arunachal Pradesh also.
- Important locations where oil is being produced in India are Digboi, Naharkatiya, Moran, Sibsagar, Badarpur and Rudrasagar in Assam region; Cambay, Kalol and Ankleshwar in Gujarat.

Nickel

- Deposits of this mineral are found in Jharkhand, Cuttack and Mayurbhanj districts of Odisha, Metallic nickel is used for mixing with iron to produce steel.

Silver

- India is rather poor in silver. Important deposits are located in the Kolar region in Karnataka and in Bihar, Tamil Nadu and Rajasthan.

Minerals for Atomic Energy

- The important minerals which are used for obtaining atomic energy are thorium, uranium and beryllium.
- Thorium is processed from the beach sands (monozite sands) found in the coastal areas in Kerala and Tamil Nadu.
- Deposits of uranium are found in Jharkhand (Jadugoda mines in Singhbhuni district), Chhattisgarh (Bastar district), Himachal Pradesh and Uttar Pradesh.

TRANSPORT AND COMMUNICATION

Transport

- The four major means of transport are the railways, roadways, waterways and airways.

Railways

- Railways are the largest public sector undertaking in the country.
- They are the most important means of transport. They carry about 75 percent of the passenger traffic and 80 percent of the freight traffic.
- Railways in India began in 1853. The first train was started between Mumbai and Thane and the total initial route length was 34 km.

- The total route length of the Indian Railways is currently over 65,000 km.
- For operational ease, the Indian Railways are divided into 16 zones. The zones and their headquarters are:

S.No.	*Zones*	*Headquarters*
1.	Central	Mumbai CST
2.	Eastern	Kolkata
3.	Northern	New Delhi
4.	North Eastern	Gorakhpur
5.	Northeast Frontier	Mallgaon (Guwahati)
6.	Southern	Chennai
7.	South Central	Secunderabad
8.	South Eastern	Kolkata
9.	Western	Churchgate, Mumbai
10.	East Central Railway	Hajipur
11.	East Coast Railway	Bhubaneswar
12.	North Central Railway	Allahabad
13.	North Western Railway	Jaipur
14.	South East Central Railway	Bilaspur
15.	South Western Railway	Hubli
16.	West Central Railway	Jabalpur

- Indian Railways has the fourth largest network in the world.

- The Railways in India operate in three gauges. They are broad gauge (1.676 m), metre gauge (one metre), and narrow gauge (0.672 m.).

Konkan Railway

- It is a 760-km long, biggest railway project in South Asia.
- It connects Maharashtra, Goa, Karnataka and Kerala on the west coast and passes through Maharashtra, Goa and Karnataka.
- It was completed in 1998 in eight years at a cost of ₹ 3,500 crore.
- Its northern terminal is Ratnagiri (Maharashtra) while the southern terminal is Mangalore (Karnataka).

Roads

- India has one of the largest road networks in the world.
- At present the country's total road length is 3.62 million kilometres.
- The present length of the National Highways in India is approx. 70,548 km. They constitute only 2% of the total road length and carry nearly 40% of the road traffic.
- The *Golden Quadrilateral Project* connecting the four Metropolitan cities of Delhi, Mumbai, Chennai and Kolkata covering a total distance of 5,952 kms is currently being processed. Also in consideration are North-South and East-West corridors (7300 km), connecting Srinagar to Kanyakumari and Silchar to Saurashtra.

Shipping

- There are 13 major ports and 200 other ports.
- The major ports situated on the west coast are Kandla (Gujarat), Mumbai, Jawaharlal Nehru (Nhava Sheva) (Maharashtra), Marmugao (Goa), New Mangalore (Karnataka), and Cochin (Kerala).
- The major ports on the eastern coast are Kolkata/ New Haldia (West Bengal); Paradip (Orissa), Visakhapatnam (AP), Chennai, Ennore and Tuticorin (Tamil Nadu).
- The Central Inland Water Transport Corporation operates services for carrying goods between Kolkata and Assam *via* Bangladesh.

Air Transport

- The organised air transport service was started in 1932, Tata Airways Limited introduced air services between Karachi and Lahore (both places now in Pakistan).
- International airports are managed by the International Airport Authority of India (IAAI) which was set up in 1972.

COMMUNICATIONS

Post and Telegraph

- The Indian postal network is the largest in the world.
- The public postal system in India was started in 1837.
- The postal department was set up much later in 1854 when nearly 700 post offices had already been func-

tioning.

- Today the number of post offices in the country is 1,54,979 and out of these 13,982 are located in rural areas and 15,797 in urban areas.
- The distribution of mail functions with the help of the PIN code (Postal Index Number code) system. These six digit codes identify the departmental post office to which a letter is to reach for delivery.
- The telex service was started in 1963.
- There are teleprinter exchanges in more than 178 cities facilitating communication all over the country
- Hindustan Teleprinters Limited, Chennai, manufactures teleprinters and ancillary equipment.

Telephones

- The era of telephone exchanges with automatic lines began in 1913 when the first exchange of this type was established at Shimla in 1913-14. The number of telephone subscribers in India was 995.9 million as on May 2012.

Internet

- Internet (in short Net) is an interworking system of computers that allows free flow of information from one part of the network to another, provided the information is packed according to certain conventions.
- Internet has spread network of computers across several nations which has been made possible by reliable telecommunication links. One can use free information provided by the Government, universities and other organisations on the Net.

- The number of Internet users in India is about 164.81 million (March 2013).
- Information courtesy Telephone Regulatory Authority of India (July 2012).
- Telecom Regulatory Authority of India (March 2013).

6

THE UNIVERSE

Solar System

- The universe began its existence by 'Big Bang' some 15 billion years ago.
- Our Solar System comprises the sun, eight planets and their satellites.
- It consists of several thousand minor planets called asteroids or planetoids and a large number of comets.
- In order of their distance from the sun, the planets of the solar system are Mercury, Venus, Earth, Mars, Jupiter, Saturn, Uranus and Neptune.

Sun

- It is considered to be the parent and the largest member of the solar system.
- Every other member of the solar system revolves round the sun.
- The sun is made up of extremely hot gases – hydrogen and helium. It gives out huge amount of heat and light.

- The average distance of the sun from the earth is 149,597,900 km and its equatorial diameter is 1,391,980 km.
- The sun's rays travel at a tremendous speed of about 300,000 kilometres per second and take eight minutes to reach earth.
- The temperature on the surface of the sun is estimated about 5,500°C.

Mercury

- It is the planet closest to the sun.
- It is also the smallest of the eight planets orbiting the sun, being nearest to the sun.
- Mercury receives the greatest amount of heat from it.
- It has no satellite.

Venus

- It is the brightest of all the planets and is slightly smaller than earth.
- It is nearest to the earth.
- It is called Morning Star or Evening Star.

Mars

- It is the first planet beyond Earth.
- Mars completes one revolution of the Sun in about 687 days.
- It rotates on its axis in 24 hours, 37 minutes and 22.663 seconds, i.e. almost the same period of time as taken by earth.
- It has two satellites.

Jupiter

- It has an equatorial diameter of 142,880 km and a polar diameter of 133,540 km.
- It is the largest planet of our solar system.
- Its outer layers are gaseous, composed of hydrogen and its compounds.
- Jupiter is said to have 16 satellites, 14 of which have been found through earth-based observatories.
- It is fifty times heavier than the earth.

Saturn

- Saturn is less dense but colder than Jupiter.
- Its specific gravity is less than that of water.
- Saturn was first discovered by Galileo.
- It has 62 satellites.

Uranus

- It is believed to be similar to Saturn and Jupiter and has the same low density as Jupiter.
- Uranus has five known satellites.
- It was discovered by Sir William Herschel on March 13, 1781.

Neptune

- Neptune has eight satellites, the largest being Triton.
- It was first discovered by J.G. Galle in 1846.

Moon

- It is the only natural satellite of the earth.
- It is also the nearest neighbour of the earth at a mean distance of 384,400 km centre-to-centre; 376,284 km surface-to-surface.

- Its diameter is 3,475 km and average orbital speed is 3,680 km per hour.
- The moon orbits the earth. Only 50 percent of the moon's surface is directly visible from the earth.
- The period of rotation of our moon is equal to its period of revolution around earth. This period is 27 days, 7 hours, 43 minutes and 11.47 seconds.
- Neil A. Armstrong and Edwin E. Aldrin Jr. of USA were the first persons to land on the moon on July 21,1969 in spaceship Apollo 11.

7

INDIAN ECONOMY

CHARACTERISTICS

Characteristics of Indian economy are:

- Under-developed Economy
- Mixed Economy
- Federal Economy

Under-developed Economy

- The Planning Commission in the First Five-Year Plan defined an Under-developed economy as one "which is characterised by the coexistence in greater or lesser degree of unutilised or under-utilised man-power on the one hand, and of unexploited natural resources on the other."

Causes of India's Under-development

- Low per capital income
- India's per capital net income (factor cost at current prices) was ₹ 40,141 in year 2008-09 which increased to ₹ 43,749 in year 2009-10; ₹ 54,835 (2010-11); and ₹ 61,564 (2011-12).

Low Rate of Capital Formation

- In India, investment is 20 percent to 25 percent of the national income whereas in the case of the USA, Canada and West Europe, it is 25 percent to 30 percent.

Shortage of Savings

- In India, savings are 20 percent to 25 percent. These are too low in the context of requirements of development.

Excessive Dependence on Agriculture

- In India about 75 percent of the people depend on agriculture.

Over-population

- According to 2011 Census, India's population is about 1,027 million and is increasing at the rate of 2.14 percent per year.

Industrial Backwardness

- Industrial development in India has been very slow and uneven. Hardly 10 percent of her total population is engaged in industry.

Under-utilisation of Natural Resources

- India is under-developed because her natural resources like water resources, forest resources and mineral resources are largely unexploited and under-utilised or under-exploited.

Unemployment and Under-employment

- India has a large and growing volume of unemployment in urban areas and "disguised unemployment" in rural areas.

- Too many persons are employed in agriculture, whose marginal productivity is zero.

Federal Economy

- As India has a federal form of government, its financial system is federal.

Economic Planning in India

Objectives of Planning in India are:

- Securing an increase in national income;
- Achieving a planned rate of investment within a given period to bring the actual investment as a proportion of National income to a higher level;
- Reducing inequality in the distribution of income and wealth;
- Providing additional employment; and
- Adopting measures to increase agricultural production, manufacturing capacity of producers and a favourable balance of payments.

THE PLANNING COMMISSION

Composition

- It was set up in March 1950.
- It consists of a Chairman, a Deputy Chairman and other members.

It is a non-statutory body. Its main functions are :

- Assessment of material, capital and human resources of the country.
- Formulation of Plans for the most effective and balanced utilisation of the country's resources.
- Definition of the nature of machinery for the

implementation of the plan in all its aspects.

- Appraisal from time to time of the progress achieved in the execution of each stage of the plan.
- Public cooperation in national development.
- Perspective planning.

National Development Council

- It comprises chief ministers of all the states and is headed by the Prime Minister.

Its main function are:

- To prescribe guidelines for the formulation of National Plan, including the assessment of resources for the plan.
- To consider the National Plan as formulated by the Planning Commission.
- To consider important questions of social and economic policy affecting national developments.
- To review the working of the plan from time to time.

INDIA'S POPULATION

Census, 2011

- India now has a population of 1.21 billion according to the latest Census figures released by the Home Secretary and the Registrar General of India on March 31. This is an increase of 181 million people since the last Census – nearly equivalent to the population of Brazil.
- India's population is now bigger than the combined population of USA, Indonesia, Brazil, Pakistan and Bangladesh, says the Census report.

- Among the States and the Union Territories, Uttar Pradesh is the most populous state with 199 million people, followed by Maharashtra with 112 million people. Lakshadweep is the least populated with 64,429 people.
- Of the total population, 623.7 million are males and 586.5 million females.
- However, population has grown at a rate of 17.64 percent which is the sharpest reduction in growth rate ever.
- The percentage decadal growth rates of the six most populous States have declined during 2001-11 compared with 1991-2011. The population growth in Uttar Pradesh has declined from 25.85 percent to 20.09 percent, in Maharashtra from 22.73 percent to 15.99 percent, in Bihar from 28.62 percent to 25.07 percent, in West Bengal from 17.77 percent to 13.93 percent, in Andhra Pradesh from 14.59 percent to 11.10 percent and in Madhya Pradesh form 24.26 percent to 20.30 percent.
- While Dadra & Nagar Haveli and Puducherry have the highest population growth rate of about 55 percent, Nagaland has the lowest. The growth rate was at its lowest between 1941-1951 when it was 13.3%, but that was a time of famine, religious killings, and the transfer of populations in the run-up to Partition. Between 1961 and 1981 population had grown alarmingly by more than 24%. The slowdown in population growth is a relief to the government, which has another reason to be happy. The density of population is highest in Delhi, followed by Chandigarh.

- The 2011 Census report also shows that India now has a child sex ratio of 914 female against 1,000 male – the lowest since Independence; while the overall sex ratio increased to 940 against 933 in the previous census.

- An increase in sex ratio was observed in 29 States/ Union Territories. Kerala with 1,084 has the highest sex ratio followed with Puducherry with 1,038. With 618, Daman & Diu has the lowest ratio. This is the highest sex ratio at the national level since Census 1971; Kashmir, Bihar and Gujarat-have shown a decline in sex ratio as compared to census 2001.

- An increasing trend in the child sex ratio was seen in Punjab, Haryana, Himachal Pradesh, Gujarat, Tamil Nadu, Mizoram and the Andaman & Nicobar Islands, but in the remaining States/UTs, the ratio showed a decline. While the overall sex ratio has improved since 1991, the decline in child sex ratio has been unabated since the 1961 Census. The total number of children in the age group of 0-6 is now 158.8 million, less by five million since 2001

- The provisional data of the 2011 census gave the country good tidings on the literacy front, as the literacy level has increased by 9.21 percentage points in the past decade to touch 74.04 percent.

- The female literacy level saw a significant jump as compared to males; the female literacy in 2001 was 53.67 percent and it has gone up to 65.46 percent in 2011. The male literacy, in comparison, rose from 75.26 to 82.14 percent.

- Kerala, with 93.91 percent, continues to occupy the top position among States as far as literacy is concerned, while Mizoram's Serchhip district (98.76 percent) and Aizawl (98.50 percent) recorded the highest literacy rates among districts, Madhya Pradesh's Alirajpur district has the lowest literacy rate of 37.22 percent as also the naxalite-affected Chhattisgarh's Bijapur district, where the literacy rate is 41.58 percent.

- Lakshadweep followed Kerala with a literacy level of 92.28 percent, while Bihar remained at the bottom of the ladder at 63.82 percent, followed by Arunachal Pradesh at 66.95 percent. Ten states and union territories, including Kerala, Lakshadweep, Mizoram, Tripura, Goa, Daman and Diu, Puducherry, Chandigarh, NCT of Delhi and Andaman and Nicobar Islands achieved a literacy rate of above 85 percent.
- The gap of 21.59 percentage points recorded between male and female literacy rates in census has reduced to 16.68 percentage points in 2011.
- A significant milestone reached in the 2011 census is the fall in the number of illiterate persons by 31,196,847. Of the total decrease in the number of illiterates, women comprise 17,122,197 and men, 14,074,650. It was also encouraging to note that out of a total of 217,700,941 literates added during the decade, females outnumbered males by 110,069,001 to 107,631,940.
- For the first time ever, the number of people made literate in India is more than the number added to its population. Consequently, there has been a net decline of over 31 million in the total number of illiterates in the country.

- The provisional numbers point to a healthy trend. An increase of nine percentage points in the overall literacy rate for a decade is praiseworthy. We now have to see whether this is mainly because of better enrolment in primary education and lower dropout rates or because of adult literacy drives.
- The census of 2011 was conducted in two phases: house-listing and housing census, and population enumeration. An estimated 2.7 million officials had fanned out across the country to undertake the mammoth exercise that cost the government ₹ 22,000 million.
- The decadal exercise, the 15th headcount of India's population since 1872 is undertaken to create a database on demography, economic activity, literacy and education, housing and household amenities, urbanisation, fertility and mortality, social structure, language, religion and migration.
- This is the 15th Census conducted since 1872. It was carried out in two phases, covering 640 districts and 5924 subdistricts.

CENSUS 2011

Sr. No	State	Population	Growth Rate
	India	1210193422	17.64
1	Uttar Pradesh	199581477	20.09
2	Maharashtra	112372972	15.99
3	Bihar	103804637	25.07
4	West Bengal	91347736	13.93
5	Andhra Pradesh	84665533	11.10

Sr. No	State	Population	Growth Rate
6	Madhya Pradesh	72597565	20.30
7	Tamil Nadu	72138958	15.60
8	Rajasthan	68621012	21.44
9	Karnataka	61130704	15.67
10	Gujarat	60383628	19.17
11	Odisha	41947358	13.97
12	Kerala	33387677	4.86
13	Jharkhand	32966238	22.34
14	Assam	31169272	16.93
15	Punjab	27704236	13.73
16	Chhattisgarh	25540196	22.59
17	Haryana	25353081	19.90
18	Delhi	16753235	20.96
19	Jammu & Kashmir	12548926	23.71
20	Uttarakhand	10116752	19.17
21	Himachal Pradesh	6856509	12.87
22	Tripura	3671032	14.87
23	Meghalaya	2964007	27.82
24	Manipur	2721756	18.65
25	Nagaland	1980602	-0.47
26	Goa	1457723	8.17
27	Arunachal Pradesh	1382611	25.92

Sr. No	State	Population	Growth Rate
28	Puducherry	1244464	27.72
29	Mizoram	1091014	22.78
30	Chandigarh	1054686	17.10
31	Sikkim	607688	12.36
32	Andaman and Nicobar Islands	379944	6.68
33	Dadra and Nagar Haveli	342853	55.50
34	Daman & Diu	242911	53.54
35	Lakshadweep	64429	6.23

Causes of Over-population

Several causes account for this rapid increase of population.

- Almost all men and women of marriageable age enter into wedlock, leading to reproductive activity.
- The practice of early marriage gives a longer span for reproductive activity.
- Also, the tropical climate in India makes for earlier puberty.
- Grinding poverty is another influence working in the direction of high birth rate. A poor man welcomes further addition to his family in the hope of more earnings.
- Fatalism has gone so far as to create the belief that every extra mouth brings its own luck.
- Lack of education and ignorance contributes to the

same thing. People have no enjoyment or recreation, leading to greater inclination towards physical pleasures.

Remedial Measures

- A proper population policy should be two-fold.

  First, it should aim at a quick economic development.

  Second, it should aim at controlling the rate of multiplication of the existing population.

POVERTY AND UNEMPLOYMENT

Unemployment

Kinds of Unemployment

- Disguised unemployment, which means that more persons are employed in doing a job than are actually necessary.
- In the absence of good irrigation arrangements, most lands raise only one crop giving occupation to the agriculturists for only part of the year.
- In the urban areas, there is unemployment among the educated middle class because of a defective system of education and their love for "white-collar" jobs.
- There is also industrial unemployment due to rationalisation of industries.

Causes

- **Insufficient Growth of Development:** The opportunities of employment have not kept pace with the addition to labour force of the country, which is taking place as a result of the rapidly increasing population.

- **Rapid Rate of Population Growth:** It is estimated that at 1.93 percent annual rate of population increases, about 4 million fresh entrants are being added to labour force.
- **Increasing Output from Indian Universities:** The galloping rate at which mass production of matriculates, graduates and post-graduates is going on in the Indian universities, is another cause of increasing gap between employment opportunities and employment seekers in the category of educated middle class.
- **Backward Character of Indian Agriculture:** The pressure of population on land and the backward nature of our farming, agriculture cannot provide employment opportunities for the numerous rural population.

Poverty

- **Poverty Line:** *Poverty Line* is found at the level of income at which a person or a family can barely subsist with the consumption of 2400 calories in urban areas or 2200 calories in rural areas.

Causes

- **Under-development:** As the Indian economy is under-developed, the levels of her national and per capita income are low.
- **Over-population and its Rapid Growth:** The rapid growth of population is another important cause of prevailing poverty.

- **Low Agricultural Productivity:** Because of primitive techniques, small agricultural holdings, insufficient irrigation and ignorance of modern agricultural inputs, agricultural productivity is very low in India.

Strategies to Remove Poverty

- **Acceleration of Economic Growth:** The greater the growth rate, the larger are the number of employment opportunities. And the expansion in employment opportunities will help removing poverty.
- **Rural Public Works:** To provide employment to the rural people, rural public works should be started on an extensive scale.
- **Agricultural Growth on Labour Intensive Lines:** Reckless mechanisation of agriculture, which destroys more employment opportunities than it creates, should be discouraged.
- **Land Reforms:** By imposing ceiling on land-holdings and their effective implementation, a good amount of land can be acquired to be distributed among the landless labourers.
- **Rural Industrialisation:** Rural industries, with their small scale and simple technology, offer much greater opportunities for employment.
- **Population Control:** Unless there is control on population, any further wealth generation will be depleted before utilisation.

8

SCIENCE AND TECHNOLOGY

Science Policy in India

- India's Science Policy outlined in the form of a resolution was passed in 1958, to secure for the people of India, the benefits from the acquisition of scientific knowledge and its application.
- Following the recommendations of the Sarkar Committee, the Government established five Indian Institutes of Technology (IITs) – at Kharagpur, Bombay (Mumbai), Madras (Chennai), Kanpur and Delhi within a decade. Now its number has been increased to 13.
- The IITs are premier institutions for technological research in India and work in close consultation with the industry.

India's Nuclear Policy

- Nuclear energy must be used for peaceful purposes.
- Nuclear weapons must be eliminated from all over the world.
- India will not even undertake peaceful explosions unless it is absolutely necessary.

- India will keep her nuclear options open and not sign the Nuclear Non-Proliferation Treaty so long as it is discriminatory.

India's Space Achievements

- There have been several achievements over the last two decades with the launching of Aryabhata on April 19, 1975.
- Till end-2010, 53 satellites have been launched.
- All these satellites were designed and fabricated in India.

INDIAN SPACE MISSION

ARYABHATA	19-04-75	Scientific
BHASKARA-I	07-06-79	Earth observations
ROHINI	10-08-79	Earth observations
ROHINI-I	18-07-80	Earth observations
ROHINI-II	31-05-81	Scientific
APPLE	19-06-81	Communication
BHASKARA-II	20-11-81	Earth observations
INSAT-1A	10-04-82	Multipurpose
ROHINI	17-04-83	Scientific
INSAT-1B	30-08-83	Multipurpose
SROSS-1	24-03-87	Technology
IRS-1A	17-03-88	Remote sensing
SROSS-II	13-07-88	Technology
INSAT-1C	21-07-88	Multipurpose
INSAT-ID	21-06-90	Multipurpose
IRS-IB	12-06-91	Remote sensing
SROSS-III	29-08-92	Scientific

INSAT-2A	10-07-92	Multipurpose
INSAT-2B	23-07-93	Multipurpose
IRS-1E	20-09-93	Remote sensing
SROSS-IV	04-05-94	Scientific
IRS-P2	15-10-94	Remote sensing
INSAT-2C	07-12-95	Telecom
IRS-1C	28-12-95	Remote sensing
IRS-P3	21-03-96	Remote sensing
INSAT-2D	04-06-97	Telecom
IRS-1D	29-09-97	Remote sensing
INSAT-2E	03-04-99	Multipurpose
INSAT-3B	22-03-00	Telecom
GSAT-I	28-03-01	Communication
GSAT-II	18-04-01	Communication
GSAT-III	08-05-03	Communication
INSAT-3C	24-01-02	Telecom
METSAT	12-09-02	Indigenous Success
INSAT-3A	10-04-03	Telecom
INSAT-3E	29-09-03	Communication
RESOURCESAT-1	17-10-03	Remote Sensing
EDUSAT	20-09-04	Educational
HAMSAT	5-05-05	Radio Communication
INSAT-4C	9-09-06	Communication
CARTOSAT-2	10-01-07	Communication
SRE-1	10-01-07	Recovery experiment
INSAT-4B	12-03-07	Communication
AGILE (Italian)	23-04-07	Scientific

INSAT-4CR	02-09-07	Communication
CARTOSAT-2A	28-04-08	-
TECSAR(Israel)	21-01-08	Spy Satellite
CHANDRAYAAN-I	22-10-08	Moon observation
WZM	21-12-08	Communication Satellite
RISAT-2 (Radar imaging satellite)	20-04-09	Surveillance Satellite
OCEANSAT-2	23-09-09	Multipurpose
GSAT-4	15-04-010	-
CARTOSAT-2B, ALSAT-2A, NLS-6.1 & 6.2, STUDSAT	12-07-010	Nano and Pico Satellites
GSAT-5P,	25-12-010	-
RESOURCESAT-2	20-04-011	-
GSAT-8/INSAT-4G	21-05-011	Communications
GSAT-12	15-07-011	Communications
Megha-Tropiques	12-10-011	Weather

INDIA'S MISSILE PROGRAMME

- An Integrated Guided Missile Development Programme was launched by India in 1983. It comprises following missiles developed by DRDO.

Guided and Ballistic Missiles

- Prithvi: It is a short range, surface-to-surface battlefield tactical missile having a range of 150 km with 1,000 kg warhead and 250 km with 500 kg warhead.
- Trishul : It is short range, surface-to air-missile having a range of 500 m to 9 km.

- Akash: It is a medium range, surface-to air missile having a range of 25 km.
- Agni I and Agni II: In order to strengthen the Indian Armed Forces, India once more tested its indigenous missile.
- Agni II missile from Chandipur in Balasore, Odisha, successfully launched on January 25, 2002. Agni-I, Agni-II with range of 1,500 km and 2,000 km, respectively.
- Dhanush: It is a naval version of Prithvi missile. Dhanush can strike surface-to-surface up to 150 to 300 nautical miles.
- Nag: It is a third generation "fire and forget" antitank guided missile having a range of 4 km.
- MBT-Arjun: It is India's Main Battle Tank (MBT), indigenously designed and developed by DRDO and Combat Vehicle Research Development Establishment (CVRDE), Avadi.
- The Arjun weighs 58 tonnes and hence falls in main battle tank category (above 50 tonnes).
- Lakshya: The Pilotless Target Aircraft (PTA), Lakshya, is a sophisticated unmanned aircraft.
- Pinaka: To build up ground support for Indian Army, it is a mobile weapon system characterised by capability to fire up to 12 rockets within a second.
- Nishant: Earlier called Falcon, is India's indigenous Remotely Piloted Vehicle (RPV).
- It can carry a 45 kg payload, travel at a speed of 150 kmp/hour and fly for more than five hours.

Scientific Instruments

- Ammeter: It is used to measure the strength of electric current in amperes.

- Air Cooler: It is an apparatus for cooling the air. Here, air is blown through water and is thus cooled.
- Amniocentesis: It is a pre-natal diagnostic procedure administered on pregnant women to detect the increasing number of diseases in foetus. It can be used for determining the sex status of the foetus also.
- Altimeter: It is an instrument used in aircraft for measuring altitudes.
- Anemometer: It is an instrument for measuring the speed, direction and strength of wind.
- Bakelite: It is an artificially prepared practical insulator. It is commercially used in the manufacture of switches, plugs.
- Barometer: This is an instrument for measuring atmospheric pressure.
- Beaufort Scale: It is used to measure wind force.
- Binocular, Prism: It is an instrument for seeing distant objects more distinctly. It has a high magnifying power and can cover a much wider field of view.
- Black Box: It is a flight-recorder self-contained unit of electronic circuitry which records data on the functioning of an aircraft and its system.
- Burette: It is a graduated glass with a top used for measuring the volume of liquid run out of it. It is used in volumetric analysis.
- Carburettor: It is used for mixing air with petrol and vapour in the internal combustion engine.
- Cardiograph: It is an instrument for tracing the heart beats on paper.
- Chronometer: It is an accurate time measuring instrument kept on board ships.

- Clinical Thermometer: This is a thermometer used for measuring temperature of human bodies. Its range is 35° C to 43° C. The normal temperature of human body is 37.2° C.
- Computer: It is a data-processing machine which stores information according to requirement. It was invented by Eckert Manchly of England in 1946.
- Cryogenic Engine: It is used for sending up geostationary satellites to receive scientific information.
- Cyclotron: It is an apparatus for smashing atoms.
- Davy's Safety Lamp: It is used in mines to prevent explosion. The heat of the flames being conducted by wire gauze, the gas outside is kept below ignition point.
- Diode: It is a 2-electrode vacuum tube consisting of a cathode that emits electrons by thorium emission and surrounded by a plate. It is used as a rectifier to convert AC into DC.
- Dynamo: It is an instrument for transforming mechanical energy into electrical energy.
- Dynamometer: It is an instrument for measuring current from a dynamo.
- Electric Motor: It converts mechanical energy into electrical energy.
- Electroencephalograph (EEG): It is a machine for recording the electric currents passing through the brain. It is used in determining brain diseases.
- Electrometer: It is an instrument for determining the influence of electric potential.
- Electron Microscope: It is an instrument similar in purpose to the ordinary light microscope but with

a much greater magnifying power (about 10,000 times). In this, instead of a beam of light to illuminate the object, a parallel beam of electrons is focussed by magnetic lens. It is employed to determine the composition of crystals.

- Eudiometer: It is a glass tube for measuring volume changes in chemical reactions between gases.
- Eye Glass: It is an instrument applied to eyes to see magnified images of small objects.
- Fathometer: It is an instrument for measuring the depth of sea in fathoms.
- Fuse: It is a wire of tin and lead with low melting point and high resistance. With high currents, the wire melts and the circuit breaks without damaging the main installation.
- Galvanometer: It is an instrument for detecting feeble currents.
- Geiger Counter: It is an instrument to measure radioactivity.
- Gyroscope: It is fitted as stabiliser in ships and torpedoes.
- Hydrometer: It is an instrument for determining the specific gravity of liquids. It is usually in the form of a glass bulb.
- Hygrometer: It is an instrument for measuring the amount of water vapour present in atmosphere.
- Internal Combustion Engine: It is the engine in which combustion takes place within the cylinder. It was invented by Rudolf Diesel.
- Iron Lung: It is an apparatus for producing artificial respiration.

- Lactometer: It is an apparatus for measuring the purity of milk.
- Lightning Conductor: It is a device which is used to protect high buildings from the destructive effects of lightning.
- Megaphone: It is an instrument for carrying sound over long distances. In it, sound waves are converted into electrical waves and then reconverted into sound waves after transmission.
- Microphone: It renders sound audible and also raises its pitch. It converts sound energy into electrical energy.
- Microscope: it is an instrument for observation of small minute objects. It was invented by Berliner.
- Modem: It is a device linking a computer system with others so that data can be transmitted at high speed from one computer to another.
- Nuclear Reactor: It is an atomic furnace wherein nuclear fission takes place. It is employed for the manufacture of radio isotopes and also for carrying research for the peaceful uses of atomic energy. It harnesses nuclear energy by controlled chain reaction.
- Oscillograph: It is an instrument to record on a film the oscillations of an electric current.
- Pager: It is a one-way wireless communication device to receive messages.
- Periscope: It is an instrument which enables the crew of a submarine to obtain survey of ships, etc., on the surface of the sea when the submarine itself is submerged in water.

- Photometer: It is an instrument for comparing the intensity of illumination of two objects.
- Polygraph (Lie Detector): It detects the changes in pulse rate or respiration in the body.
- Pyrometer: It is an instrument for recording high temperature from a distance.
- RADAR (Radio Detecting and Ranging): It is an instrument for detecting the presence of enemy aircraft, submarines, etc., and for determining their direction, distance and speed.
- Rectifier: It is a device to convert AC current into DC current.
- Richter Scale: It is a scale for measuring the intensity of an earthquake. It was developed by Charles F. Richter in 1935. The strength of an earthquake is indicated by the number called Richter magnitude which is obtained from an instrument called Seismograph.
- Robot: It is a machine that resembles a human being and does mechanical routine tasks on command.
- Rocket: It is a metal case that can be projected to any height or distance by the force of explosives it contains. It works on the principle of *Conservation of Linear Momentum.*
- Salinometer: It is an instrument for measuring the concentration of salt in water.
- Seismometer: It is an apparatus for measuring the intensity of earthquake shocks.
- Sextant: It is an optical instrument used for finding out the altitude of celestial bodies and their angular distance. The invention is attributed to John Hadley.

- SONAR: It is the device for detecting submarines in the sea.
- Spectrometer: It is an instrument by means of which the angular deviation of ray of light produced by a prism can be determined.
- Sphygomomanometer: It is an instrument for measuring blood pressure.
- Stethoscope: It is a sound-magnifying instrument used by doctors for listening to the sound produced by heart and lungs.
- Submarine: It is a ship which ordinarily floats on water but when required can be submerged in water. This is done by varying the density.
- Tachometer: It is an instrument for measuring the speed of rotation.
- Telestar: It is an instrument to transmit wireless or television broadcasts more distinctly across continents *via* space.
- Theodolite: It is an instrument for measuring angles of elevation and depression. It is used by surveyors.
- Thermoplastics: These are heat resistance plastic objects.
- Thermostat: It is an instrument which controls temperature automatically. It is used in refrigerators, heaters, geysers.
- Torpedo: It is a cigar-shaped self-propelling missile that can be aimed at a ship and it explodes on touching it and makes a hole at the bottom of the ship.
- Transformer: It is an electric apparatus which is used to convert high voltage into low voltage and vice versa.

- Transistor: It is a semi-conductor device which is capable of amplification. It is made of silicon.
- Turbines: They are horizontal water wheels propelled by steam, air or water. These produce power for the propulsion of ships for generating electricity. Now a days gas turbines have also come into prominence.
- Voltmeter: It is an instrument for measuring the potential difference across two points of an electrical circuit.
- World Wide Web (WWW): It is the most exciting of Internet activity when on the click of the mouse, one can have access to information easily. It has revolutionised the world by enabling connection of millions of computers around the world.

NUTRIENTS

Carbohydrates

- Carbohydrates are mainly compounds of carbon, hydrogen and oxygen.
- These are produced by green plants during photo-synthesis.
- Carbohydrates are known as saccharides or com-pounds containing sugar.
- The simplest carbohydrates are the simple sugars or monosaccharides. For instance, glucose, fructose, galactose, etc.
- Glucose is the most important sugar occurring in animals.
- Fructose is the most common form of sugar found in fruits.

- Disaccharides are compounds of two monosacchariedes. A molecule of sucrose is formed from a molecule of glucose and one of fructose.
- Lactose or milk sugar is found in human milk and cow's milk. It is formed by a glucose molecule and a galactose.
- Cells draw glucose from blood and oxidise it for obtaining energy.

Lipids

- These are made of carbon, hydrogen and sometimes oxygen.
- Lipids are insoluble in water.
- Fatty acids are called saturated if they do not have any double bonds between the carbon of the molecular chain. For instance, palmitic acid, steraic acid, etc.
- Fats that are generally liquids at room temperature are called oils. Oils are rich in unsaturated fatty acids.
- Such oils are recommended by physicians for patients who suffer from high blood cholesterol or cardiovascular diseases.
- During hydrogenation, the unsaturated acids get saturated and the oil becomes a solid fat, e.g. Vanaspati ghee and margarine.
- Waxes are another class of lipids. They form water insoluble coatings on hair and skin in animals; stems, leaves and fruits of plants.
- Cholesterol is also the precursor of hormones such as progesterone, testosterone, etc.
- Cholesterol and its ester are insoluble in water and are deposited in the arteries and veins if the blood

cholesterol rises. This leads to high blood pressure and heart diseases.

- Fats deposited beneath the skin and around the internal organs minimise loss of body heat and also act as cushions to absorb mechanical impacts.

Amino Acids

- These are made of carbon, hydrogen, oxygen and nitrogen and in some cases, also sulphur.
- When a few amino acids are joined together, the molecule is called a peptide.
- Their principal function is building blocks for proteins.

Nucleotides

- They contain, hydrogen, oxygen, nitrogen and phosphorus.
- Ribonucleotides are the basic units of ribouncleic acids (RNA) and deoxyri bonucleic acids (DNA).
- Nicotinamide and riboflavin nucleotides act as co-enzymes of oxidising enzymes.

Minerals

- Minerals are found in living oranisms as components of organic and inorganic molecules and ions.
- Calcium imparts strength and rigidity to bones and teeth by getting deposited in them along with phosphates.

Proteins

- Proteins are linear polymers of amino acids.
- Keratin protein is the major constituent of hair, skin, nails, feathers and wool.

- In plants, proteins are found in the walls of pollen grains.
- In a body fluid, haemoglobin (in blood) transports and myoglobin (in muscle) stores oxygen.
- In plants P-protein is involved in the transport of organic compounds through phloem.
- Hormones such as insulin and parathyroid hormone are proteins that regulate metabolism.
- Antibodies that participate in the defence mechanism of the body are also proteins.

Nucleic Acids

- Deoxyribonucleic Acid (DNA) is found mainly in the nucleus, but also occurs in chloroplasts and mitochondria. It is the genetic material.
- Ribonucleic Acid (RNA) is produced mostly in the nucleus, but moves out into the cytoplasm. RNA is responsible for transmitting the information from the nucleus to the ribosomes where protein synthesis takes place.
- DNA is the only molecule that can replicate itself.
- Certain animal and all plant viruses have RNA as the hereditary material.

Vitamins

- Vitamin A: It is a general health giving vitamin and it increases resistance to infection and tones up the whole system. Its deficiency causes night blindness, disorders of skin, stomach growth and respiratory diseases.
- Vitamin B: It is present in cereals, peas and beans. It protects the body from nerve diseases such as beri beri, pellagra, etc., and enlargement of liver and

adrenals. It is also called thiamine. It is considered to be hormone.

- Vitamin C: It ensures healty teeth, bones and protects the body against scurvy. It is present in fresh vegetables, orange, lemon lettuce, tomato, cabbage, turnip, potato and mango. It is water soluble. It is also called Ascorbic Acid.
- Vitamin D: It is present in milk, butter, ghee, cod liver oil, yolk of eggs and it is also produced under the skin by the rays of the sun. It helps bone promotion and prevents *rickets.*
- Vitamin E: It has vital influence on organ reproduction. Its absence causes sterility. It is present in germinating wheat. It is also call Alpha-tecopherol.

HUMAN BODY ORGAN SYSTEM

Skeleton System

- The human body is supported on a skeleton consisting of 206 long, short and irregular bones. These are together in several modes. The main functions of the skeleton are:
- To stiffen the body;
- To provide levers upon which muscles of the body work;
- To give shape to the body; and
- To protect the internal organs.

Muscular System

- Shape of the muscles are thick at the centre and thin at the ends.
- There are over 300 muscles in a human body.

These are of two types:

- Voluntary Muscles

  These are under our control, such as muscles of head, legs, neck, etc. These cause the external movements of the body.

- Involuntary Muscles

  These muscles act without our concious control.

  These are situated on the wall of the internal organs.

Circulatory System

This consists of heart and blood vessels which, by carrying blood to all parts of the body, supply nourishment to the various tissues; and by bringing it back, remove the waste products of the body.

- Heart pumps the blood to arteries which supply it to various body parts.
- In the substance of every organ, the arteries divide into a very fine network of extremely small hair-like tubes called capillaries.
- Through the walls of capillaries, the organs receive nourishment.
- The capillaries reunite and pour the blood into *veins* which carry the blood containing waste products back to the heart.
- The impure blood gathers from all parts of the body on the right auricle of the heart, from where it is sent to lungs where it is purified by the oxygen breathed in.
- The purified blood then goes to the left-hand side of the heart. Finally blood is back from where it started.

- The process goes on again and again till the last breath.

Heart

- The heart is a muscular conical organ located in the rib case between the two lungs.
- Its weight is about 300 gm in males and 200 gm in females.
- The heart is divided into four chambers. The two lower chambers are called ventricles.
- The right auricle receives the impure blood and left auricle receives pure blood.
- The left ventricle pumps pure blood to various parts of body through the aorta.
- When the ventricles are full of blood, this condition is called diastole. The contracted condition of the ventricle is called systole.
- The diastole and systole alternates and this is called the heartbeat.
- A healthy human heart beats 70-80 times in a minute.
- The blood is forced out of the heart, this can be felt in the artery near the wrist. This is called the pulse (70-80 in one minute).
- The pulse is recorded by stethoscope.

Functions of the Heart

The functions of the heart are:

- To supply pure blood to all parts of the body;
- To collect impure blood from the organs of the body; and
- To pump impure blood into the lungs for purification.

Functions of the Lungs

The main functions of the lungs are:

- To purify the blood, i.e. to separate the carbon di-oxide and water vapours from blood; and
- To give oxygen to the blood.

Digestive System

- It consists of a very long (31 feet) tube, known as alimentary canal.
- Its main parts are mouth, gullet, stomach, small and large intestines. The digestive fluids saliva, gastric juice, bile and intestinal juices are poured into the canal by the neighbouring glands and walls of the tubes itself while the food is passing through various regions.
- The objective of digestion is to convert the food into a fluid state so that it is capable of being absorbed by the blood.

Saliva

- It is secreted by the three pairs of salivary glands situated in the mouth.
- It is alkaline in reaction and contains a ferment which converts starch into sugar.

Gastric Juice

- It is secreted by gastric glands in the stomach.
- It converts insoluble proteins into soluble peptones and coagulates milk.

Stomach

Its main functions are:

- To stop the action of saliva, a juice which converts starch into sugar;
- To change insoluble proteins into soluble peptones; and
- To coagulate milk.

Bile Fluid

- It is a greenish alkaline fluid poured into duodenum (part of small intestines) by the liver through the gall bladder.
- It is antiseptic and emulsifies fats.

Pancreatic Juice

- It is secreted by pancreas which are situated in the bend of duodenum.
- It secretes insulin which acts upon the carbohydrates, fats and proteins.
- It digests food and keeps the sugar balance in the body.

Liver

- It is dark red in colour and weighs about 40 to 60 ounces. It is the largest gland in the body.
- It helps in digesting food. Its main function are:
  - To act as a store of digested sugar for use when required in the body;
  - To help in digesting food;
  - To separate nitrogenous waste; and
  - To kill poisons produced in the body.

Respiratory System

- The respiratory system in the human body is an apparatus to get oxygen into the blood and carbon dioxide out of it.

- The system consists of two lungs and the passages leading to lungs, a nose and wind pipe.
- When the diaphragm contracts, a large cavity is formed in the throat.
- In order to fill up that cavity, fresh air from the nostrils is sucked in and this is called respiration.
- Then the diaphragm comes to its real form and cavity becomes smaller and we exhale the impure air and expiration takes place.

Excretory System

- Kidneys and skin are the chief organs of excretion.
- These throw the waste products out of the body in the form of urine and sweat, respectively.
- Kidneys are two in number.
- These filter the nitrogenous wastes of the body from the blood and throw them out in the form of urine.

Nervous System

- The system consists of nerves, brain and the spinal cord.
- They control the working of the various organs of the body.
- The brain controls thought, memory, intelligence, etc.
- The spinal cord controls the reflex action and works when the brain is asleep.
- Cerebrum: It is the seat of memory coordination and intelligence in the brain. It is the largest part of the brain.

Reproductive System

- There are certain organs in the body which are set apart for the reproduction of the species.
- These are of different types in males and females.

Sex Determination

- Sex chromosomes determine the sex in human beings.
- In males, there are 44 + XY chromosomes, whereas, in females there are 44 + XX.
- The number 44 represents autosomes and X and Y chromosomes determine the sex in human beings.
- The sex is established at the time of fertilisation. If male gamete with y chromosome fuse with female gamete with X chromosome, the zygote will have XY chromosome and the child born would be a male.
- If male gamete with X chromosome fuse with female gamete having X chromosome, the zygote will have XX chromosomes and the child born would be a female.

Blood

- Blood is a connective tissue which is made to circulate by the muscular pumping organ, the heart.
- In an average adult human being, there is 5.5 to 6 litres of blood.
- Plasma (fluid part of blood) consists of RBC, WBC and blood platelets.

Red Blood Corpuscles (RBC)

- Red Blood Corpuscles (RBC) or Erythrocytes' number is about 5 to 5.5 million in 1 ml of blood.

The total number is about 30 billion. Each RBC is devoid of nucleus.

- RBCs contain haemoglobin that consists of globin and Fe^{2+}, i.e., heme.
- 100 ml of blood contains 15 mg of haemoglobin. An individual may suffer from anaemia if the haemoglobin is lesser than this specified amount.
- Haemoglobin carries oxygen to different cells of the body and brings carbon dioxide from the cells.
- Life span of RBCs is 120 days.

White Blood Corpuscles (WBC)

- The number of leukocytes is 5000-6000 in one ml of blood.
- The total number of WBCs is about 75 million.
- The number of leukocytes increases in infections like pneumonia, blood cancer (Leukaemia), etc.
- These contain nucleus.

Platelets

- These are small and without nuclei.
- Their number varies from 0.15 to 0.45 million in one ml of blood.
- Their normal life span is one week.
- These help in blood clotting at the site of injury by liberating thromboplastin.

Blood Pressure

- The normal blood pressure of a person is 120/80 mm of Hg.
- During contracted or systolic condition, it is 120 and during diastolic, it is 80.

- The maximum normal blood pressure is 150 in males and 140 in females.
- The blood pressure is measured by sphygmomanometer.

Arteries

- Blood flows from the heart to the body.
- Mostly oxygenated blood flows through the arteries except in pulmonary artery.

Veins

- Blood flows from body organs to the heart.
- Mostly deoxygenated blood flows through the veins except in pulmonary vein.

Gene

- It is a unit of hereditary information and is responsible for inheritance from one generation to the next.
- A little bit or a segment of DNA is called gene.

DISEASES

Diseases Caused by Bacteria

- Diphtheria, Pneumonia, Tuberculosis, Plague or Bubonic Plague, Tetanus, Typhoid, Cholera, Bacillary dysentery, Whooping cough, Gonorrhoea, Syphilis, Leprosy.

Diseases Caused by Viruses

- Chickenpox, Smallpox, Common cold, Influenza flu, Measles (Rubella), Mumps, Viral Encephalitis, Pollomyelitis, Rabies (Hydrophobia), Dengue fever, Acquired Immuno Deficiency Syndrome (AIDS), etc.

9

SPORTS

Sports Terms

- Baseball: Putout, strike, home, binting.
- Badminton: Mixed double, deuce, drop, smash, let.
- Basketball: Fast break, pivot.
- Billiards: Cire, jigger, in baulk, in of carom, cannon.
- Boxing: Slam, knock-out, hitting below the belt, uppercut, kidney punch.
- Chess: Bishop, gambit, checkmate, stalemate.
- Cricket: Creases, stumped; the break; bye; leg-bye; chamber; googly; hat-trick; maiden over; drive; bowling; duck; follow on; no ball; leg break; gulley; silly point; cover point; hit-wicket; late-cut; slip; off-spinner; leg-spinner; in-swing; outswing; stone walling; chinaman, LBW.
- Football: Penalty kick (or goal kick); corner-kick; free-kick; dribble; throw-in; touch-down; stopper.
- Golf: Caddie, links, putting the green, bunker, niblic, hole.
- Hockey: Penalty stroke, sudden-death, tie-breaker,

carried; short corner; bully; sticks; offside; roll in; striking circle; under-cutting; dribble.

- Horse racing: Dead heat, jockey, punter, also ran.
- Polo: Bunker, mallet, chukker.
- Tennis: Half volley, hand, deuce, service, let, grand slam, double fault, lob, foot fault.

Measurements of courts

- Baseball: Diamond-shaped ground, 90 feet on each side and 127 feet along the diagonals.
- Badminton: 44 feet by 20 feet (for doubles) 44 feat by 17 feet (for singles).
- Billiards Table : 10 feet long, 5 feet wide and 3 feet high.
- Cricket pitch: Rectangular area – 20.12m long and 3.05m wide; popping crease – 1.22m in front of the stumps.

CUPS AND TROPHIES

International

America's Cup	Yacht Racing
Canada Cup	Golf (World Championship)
Corbillion Cup	World Table Tennis (Women)
Davis Cup	Lawn Tennis (Men)
The Derby	Horse Racing (England)
Grand National	Horse Steeple Chase Race (England)
Hopman Cup	Hardcourt Tennis
Prince of Wales Cup	Golf (England)

World Soccer Cup	Soccer
Reliance Cup	Cricket
Ryder Cup	Golf (England)
Schneider Cup	Seaplane Race (U.K.)
Thomas Cup	Badminton
Tunku Abdul Rahman	Badmiton (Asian)
U Thant Cup	Table Tennis
Uber Cup	World Badminton (Women)
Walker Cup	Golf
Winchester Cup	Polo (England)
Wimbledon Trophy	Lawn Tennis
ICC Cricket World Cup	Cricket
World Cup	Hockey

National

Aga Khan Cup	Hockey (Women)
Bombay Gold Cup	Hockey
Duleep Trophy	Cricket
Durand Cup	Football
Ezra Cup	Polo
Irani Cup	Cricket
Jaswant Singh Trophy	Best Service Sportsman
Jayalakshmi Cup	National Table Tennis Championship (Women)
Maharaja Ranjit Singh	Hockey Gold Cup
Maulana Azad Trophy	Inter-University Sports
Nehru Cup	Hockey

Nehru Trophy	Football
Nizam Gold Cup	Hockey
Radha Mohan Cup	Polo
Ranji Trophy	Cricket
Rene Frank Trophy	International Tournament for Hockey
Rovers Cup	Football
Santosh Trophy	Football
Scindia Gold Cup	Polo
Sheesh Mahal Trophy	Cricket
Subroto Mukerji Cup	Football
Wellington Trophy	Boat Rowing

10

CULTURAL ACTIVITIES

CLASSICAL DANCES

Bharatnatyam

- Enunciated in Bharat's *Natya Shastra*.
- It has survived in the precincts of south Indian temples.
- Its present form was evolved in Tanjore by Ponniah Pillai and brothers.
- Rukmani Devi gave it a new life and respectability.

Kathakali

- This dance form is from Kerala which is more dramatic than narrative in form.

Kathak

- It flourished in the north Indian princely states and was patronised by their rulers.

Kuchipudi

- This classical dance form of Andhra had its origin in the 17th century in Kuchipudi, a village in Andhra Pradesh.

Mohini Attam

- This dance of Kerala is the heir to Devedasi dance, just like Bharatnatyam, Odissi and Kuchipudi.

Manipuri

- It originated from Manipur. This is a religious dance form with Radha and Krishna being central to its themes.

Odissi

- This classical dance form of Odisha dates back to the 17th century and is performed by both males and females.

Yakshagana

- It is an all-male dance drama of Karnataka which includes music, dialogues and prose in its performance.

Folk Dance

- Some of the important folk dances and the place where these are most commonly performed are as follows:

Gidda	Punjab
Garba	Gujarat
Rass	Gujarat
Bhangra	Punjab
Kummi	Tamil Nadu and Kerala
Chhau	Bengal
Yakshagana	Karnataka
Rengma	Nagaland
Dandia	Gujarat
Rouf	Kashmir

Oraon	Jharkhand
Kuki bamboo	Nagaland
Ghumar	Rajasthan
Tamasha	Maharashtra
Jatra	Bengal
Thali	Himachal Pradesh
Mukena	Manipur
Karagem	Tamil Nadu
Kavadi	Tamil Nadu
Koodiyattam	Kerala
Kaliyattam	Kerala

FESTIVALS OF INDIA

Major Festivals

Baisakhi

- Baisakhi is a festival celebrated on April 13, especially in Punjab, upon harvest.

Basant Panchami

- Basant Panchami falling on the fifth day of dark lunar days in Magh (February) has been observed as a festival to worship Saraswati since the Vedic and Puranic times.

Bhaiya Dooj

- This festival is observed in Kartik on the second day of the waxing moon cycle.
- This is also called Yama Dwitiya or Bhratri Dwitiya. It aims at establishing mutual affection between brother and sister.

Buddha Jayanti

- It is the auspicious day when Buddha was born. Buddhists from all over India and abroad visit Bodh Gaya and Rajgir in Bihar.

Chhath Puja

- Sun (Surya), the most revered natural element, is the object of veneration during Chhath Puja, celebrated six days after Diwali.

Diwali (Deepawali)

- It is celebrated in honour of Lord Rama's homecoming after the victory over Ravana, symbolising the victory of good over evil.

Durga Puja (September-October)

- This festival commemorates the victory of Durga, wife of Siva over a buffalo headed demon (Mahishasur).

Guru Nanak Jayanti

- This day is celebrated in reverence to the birth of Guru Nanak, born on this day in 1526.

Guru Purnima

- Guru Purnima is of great importance in relation to a guru and disciple.

Holi

- Holi, the festival of colours, is celebrated in Phalgun (March) to commemorate the killing of Hiranya-kashyap by Lord Narasimha.

Karva Chauth

- In India and Nepal, married Hindu women observe

a fast on Krishna Chaturthi of Kartik (October-November) for her husband's welfare, health and long life.

Kumbh Mela

- Kumbh Mela is a highly important festival, attended by millions of people by taking a dip in the sacred waters at Haridwar, Prayag (Allahabad), Ujjain and Nashik, observed at an interval of twelve years at Prayag.

Navaratri

- Counting a fortnight of fifteen days in the year, there are 4 Nava Ratras, out of which, Chaitr Shukl Pratipada (Vasantik) and Ashwin Shukl Pratipada (Shardiya) are quite important.

Pongal

- The harvest season brings along the festival Pongal, which literally means new rice, cooked with jaggery mainly in the rural Tamil Nadu.

Raksha Bandhan

- On the full moon day of Shravan, the annual ritual of Raksha Bandhan is observed, in which sisters tie Rakhi (considered as a sacred thread) on the wrist of their brothers.

Ramanavami

- The birthday of Lord Rama falls on the 9th day of month Chaitr (March-April).

Vishwakarma Puja

- This festival is celebrated in the new moon of September by the craftsmen.

Onam

- Onam is Kerala's most important festival of a harvest season.

Pushkar Mela

- It is a fair on the banks of the Pushker lake (Rajasthan) held in October-November.

Id-ul-Fitr

- It is the greatest festival of Muslims. It comes at the end of the Islamic month of Ramzan.

Id-ul-Azha (Bakr-Id)

- It is a festival of great rejoicing; it commemorates Hazrat Ibrahim's great test of obedience to Allah who ordered him to sacrifice the person dearest to him.

Christmas

- The festival of Christmas, celebrating the birth or nativity of Christ on December 25, is an important festival of the Christians.

Easter

- This festival is celebrated on the occasion of resurrection of Jesus Christ after the event of Crucifixation at Jerusalem.

Bhogali Bihu

- It is the Assamese harvest festival celebrated in January at the end of the winter paddy harvest.

Lohri

- The Lohri festival is celebrated in January towards the end of the winter season in Punjab and Haryana.

INDIAN MUSIC

Classical Music

- Indian classical music can be divided into two styles- Carnatic (South Indian) and Hindustani (North Indian). Both the schools of music trace their origin back to the books *Natya Shastra* and *Sangita Ratnakara.*

Carnatic Music

- The most prominent exponents of this style of music are Thyagaraja, Muttuswami Diksitar and Syama Shastri.

Raga

- The Indian raga serves as the framework of the musician based upon the several swaras; each raga has its own time, season, mood and festival.
- The raga Bhopali is for early morning, Malhar for rainy season, Maru Bihag for night, etc. There are hundreds of ragas and raginis in Indian music.

Khayal

- Amir Khusrao is supposed to be originator of this delicate romantic school of music. The theme is usually a love story sung by a woman.

Tala

- The Indian theory of tala is based on a variety of rhythms consisting of different combinations of intricate patterns.

National Calendar

- The unified National Calendar was introduced from March 22, 1957.

- It is based on Saka Era, which began with the vernal equinox of 78 AD.
- Chaitra is the first month and Phalgun is the last month.

GOVERNMENT OF INDIA INSTITUTIONS

Anthropological Survey of India

- It conducts researches to record and understand the bio-cultural diversities of India's population and to serve as information bank for national planning and development.

Archaeological Survey of India (ASI)

It was founded in 1961. Its main functions are:

- Exploration and excavation of ancient sites;
- Preservation of centrally-protected monuments and other works of art;
- Epigraphical research;
- Maintenance of archaeological museums;
- Implementation of Ancient Monuments and Archaeological Sites and Remains Act, 1958; and Antiquities and Art Treasures Act, 1972.

- The ASI has a library, which is one of the oldest in the country. It contains rare materials not only of India but also of South-East Asia and West Asia.

Bhabha Atomic Research Centre (BARC)

- It was started at Trombay near Bombay (Mumbai) in 1957.
- It is the largest single scientific establishment in the country. At present two experimental nuclear reactors are in operation at Trombay – a one

megawatt (MW) swimming pool type of reactor APSARA and a 40 MW reactor CIRUS.

- A zero energy experimental thermal reactor ZERLINA and a fast critical facility PURNIMA were used for carrying out reactor physics experiments.
- A fifth 100 MW research reactor DHRUVA was dedicated to the nation at Trombay in November 1985.

Central Board of Film Certification

- It is a statutory body constituted in 1951 for certifying films for public exhibition throughout India. It consists of a chairman and honorary non-official members. The head office of the Board is at Mumbai.

Council of Scientific and Industrial Research

- It has a network of National Laboratories and is a major agency for scientific and industrial research. It supports research in universities and other centres of learning.

Defence Research and Development Organisation (DRDO)

- The principal responsibilities of DRDO relate to the design and development of new and sophisticated weapons and equipments based on the operational requirements.
- Its main achievements include Integrated Missile Development Programme (IGMDP).

Employment Exchanges

- These were started in 1945 to resettle demolished war personnel and in 1947 were entrusted with the task of finding employment for the displaced persons and their scope was enlarged later. These give priority to the Scheduled Castes, Scheduled Tribes and retrenched Government employees.

Film and Television Institute of India (FTII)

- It was established in 1960 at Pune to impart training in the art and craft of filmmaking. Training in television was added in 1971.

Forest Survey of India

- It was set up in 1981 on the recommendation of the National Commission on Agriculture. Its main activities are forest inventory and re-inventory, photo-interpertation and mapping, data processing and training and some special studies.

Geological Survey of India (GSI)

- It was established in 1851 with headquarters in Calcutta (Kolkata). It is the principal agency entrusted with the mapping and exploration of minerals in India.

Hudco

- It stands for Housing and Urban Development Corporation. It was set up in 1970 as an apex organisation mainly to provide finance for housing and urban development programmes in the country with the primary emphasis for the persons belonging to low income groups and economically weaker sections.
- The main sources of finance of HUDCO are equity contribution by the Government borrowing from LIC and floating debentures.

Indian Council of Historical Research

- With headquarters in New Delhi, the Council enunciates and implements a national policy of historical research and encourages scientific writing of history.

Indian Council of Medical Research

- It was set up in 1911 with its headquarters in New Delhi. It conducts medical research in India through a network of research institutes and centres covering a wide spectrum.

Indian Council of Agricultural Research

- Its function is to plan, undertake, promote and co-ordinate agricultural and animal husbandry plans including research, education and field applications.
- It gives support for the setting up and development of at least one agricultural university in each State. It functions through a network of research laboratories.

Indian Institute of Forest Management

- It was set up in 1981 at Bhopal.
- It has a wide range of activities covering research, development and management needs of the social forestry and farm forestry.

Indian Council of Cultural Relations

- It was set up in 1950 for promoting Indian cultural relations with foreign exchange through bilateral cultural exchange programmes, including symposia, lectures, foreign films and festivals, etc. It administers the Nehru Award for International Understanding.

National Archives of India

- It is the largest and perhaps the best organised record repository in Asia. It has in its custody several million public records, maps, private papers, microfilms, books, occupying a total length of 25 km of shelf space. It provides research facilities to several hundred research scholars.

National Informatics Centre

- It catalyses computer usage in decision-making mechanism in various ministries and departments of the Central Government.

National Sample Survey Organisation

- It obtains comprehensive and continuing information relating to social, economic, demographic, industrial and agricultural statistics through sample surveys on countrywise basis.

National School of Drama and Asian Theatre

- It was set up in 1959 and is fully financed by the Government of India.
- The training in the school covers all aspect of theatre, which *inter-alia* includes acting, direction and production of drama. It also promotes research survey in classical, traditional and modern drama.
- The school is in touch with parallel institutions all over the world through cultural exchange programmes between India and other countries.

National Service Corps

- It was introduced in 1968. Its main purpose is to bring students in touch with real rural life, inculcating in them ideas of responsible leadership, bringing out their qualities and enabling them to help them in the process of nation building.
- Its work programme includes Scouting, Red

Cross Work, First Aid, Home Nurses and Civil Defence.

National Council of Educational Research and Training

- It assists the Union Ministry of Human Resource Development in the formulation and implementation of its policies in the field of school education.
- The Council has developed new curricula and syllabi for classes I to XII in the new (10 + 2) pattern of education.

National Dairy Development Board

- It is engaged in the development of rural life by undertaking multi-purpose activities like-animal husbandry, dairy technology, food technology, agricultural planning, nutrition, genetics, management, etc.
- It helps the villagers to develop professional capabilities they need to run their dairy factories and market their output.

Prasar Bharti

- It is a statutory autonomous corporation on the lines of BBS to control All India Radio and Doordarshan. Its Board consists of a Chairman and members and controls the affairs of Prasar Bharti.

Press Council of India

- It was set up in 1966 for safeguarding the freedom of the press and for maintaining and improving the standard of newspapers and news agencies in India.
- It is a quasi-judicial body functioning to consider complaints against newspapers and news agencies

and journalists offending against ethics and public taste.

- The Council also considers complaints from individuals, associations or newspapers against any person, group or organisation of interference with the free functioning of the Press.

Publications Division

- It brings out books, pamphlets, albums and journals to provide the common reader with information regarding diverse aspects of our national life and culture and messages of national leaders.

Unit Trust of India

- It was established by the Government of India in February, 1964 with the main objective of mobilising savings of the middle class for investment in industrial and other projects.
- It ensures a minimum return of 6 percent per annum.

Zoological Survey of India

- It carries out studies in diverse fields of animal taxonomy and investigations related to agriculture, forestry, fisheries and public health and hygiene.
- Particular emphasis is given to studies on ecological aspects.

11

MATHEMATICS

ARITHMETIC

- Natural numbers : 1,2,3,4,5,6,7,8,9.
- Integers : -9, -8, ... -1, 0, 1, 2, ... 9 are integers
- Prime numbers : 2, 3, 5, 7, 11, 13, 17, 19, 23 ... These numbers are divisible by itself only.
- Composite numbers : 4, 6, 8, 10, 12, 14, ... etc.
- Highest Common Factor (HCF) or Greatest Common Divisor (GCD) of two or more numbers is the greatest number which exactly divides the numbers.
- Lowest Common Multiple (LCM) of two or more numbers is their smallest multiple which is exactly divisible by these numbers.

LCM x HCF = Ist number x IInd number

$$\text{LCM} = \frac{\text{Ist number} \times \text{IInd number}}{\text{HCF}}$$

$$\text{HCF} = \frac{\text{Ist number} \times \text{IInd number}}{\text{LCM}}$$

BUSINESS MATHS

For the principal (P) at the rate of R% for time period T years:

Simple interest $S.I. = \frac{P \times R \times T}{100}$

Rate $R = \frac{S.I. \times 100}{P \times T}$

Time $T = \frac{S.I. \times 100}{P \times R}$

Compound Interest = Amount (A) – Principal (P)

Amount $A = P\,(1 + R/100)^T$

ALGEBRAIC FORMULAE

$(a + b)^2 = a^2 + 2\,ab + b^2$;

$a^2 + b^2 = (a+b)^2 - 2ab$;

$(a - b)^2 = a^2 - 2\,ab + b^2$;

$a^2 + b^2 = (a-b)^2 + 2ab$;

$(a + b)^3 = a^3 + b^3 + 3\,ab\,(a+b)$;

$a^3 + b^3 = (a+b)^3 - 3ab\,(a+b)$;

$(a - b)^3 = a^3 - b^3 - 3\,ab\,(a-b)$;

$a^3 - b^3 = (a-b)^3 + 3ab\,(a-b)$

MENSURATION

- Area of square of side a = a^2
- Perimeter of the square = 4a
- Diagonal of the square = $\sqrt{2a}$

- For a rectangle of length 'L' and breadth 'B',

  Area = L x B

  Perimeter = 2 (L + B)

  Diagonal = $\sqrt{L^2 + B^2}$

- For the circle of radius 'r'

  Area = πr^2

  Perimeter = $2 \pi r$

  Diameter = 2r

  $\left[\pi = \frac{22}{7}\right]$

- For the solid sphere of radius 'r'

  Surface area = $4 \pi r^2$

  Surface area of hemisphere $3 \pi r^2$

  Volume of sphere = $4/3 \pi r^3$

  Volume of hemisphere = $2/3 \pi r^3$

- Volume of cube of side 'a' = a^3
- Volume of a cuboid of length (L), breadth (B) and height (H) = $L \times B \times H$.

  Longest diagonal of the cuboid = $\sqrt{L^2 + B^2 + H^2}$

- For a cone of actual height (h) lateral heigth (l) and radius of circular base (*r*):

  Curved surface area = $\pi r l$

  Total surface area of solid cone = $\pi r (l + r)$

Volume of the cone = $1/3 \pi r^2 h$

- For a cylinder of height (h) and radius of circular ends (r):

  Curved surface area = $2 \pi rh$

  Total surface area for solid cylinder = $2 \pi r (h+r)$

  Volume of the cylinder = $\pi r^2 h$

Where $\pi = \frac{22}{7}$ /3.14

12

MISCELLANEOUS

DEFENCE FORCES

Army

- The Army is organised in six Commands—Western, Eastern, Northern, Southern, Central and Training – each under a General Officer Commanding-in-Chief of the rank of Lieutenant-General.

Border Security Force

- Its statutory functions are to promote a sense of security among the people living in the border areas.
- To prevent trans-border crimes, unauthorised entry into or exit from the territory of India.
- To prevent smuggling and any other illegal activity.

Home Guards

- It is a voluntary force formed in 1962. Its main functions are to serve as an auxiliary to the police in maintenance of law and order and help in maintaining internal security.
- To help the community in any kind of emergency

such as an air raid, fire, flood, cyclone, earthquake, epidemic.

- To help in maintenance of essential services, promote communal harmony and assist the administration in protecting weaker sections of society and perform civil defence duties.

Navy

- The Navy is organised into three Naval Commands under Flag Officers Commanding in-Chief, Western Naval Command with headquarters at Mumbai, Eastern Naval Command with headquarters at Visakhapatnam and Southern Naval Command with Headquarters at Kochi.

National Cadet Corps (NCC)

- Established in 1948, a youth organisation, entry to which is open to students of universities, colleges and schools on a voluntary basis.
- NCC consists of three Divisions – Senior, Junior and Girls.
- At the State level, the country has been divided into 16 Directorates which cover all the States and Union Territories.

Territorial Army

- It was established in 1949. It is designed to give the citizens an opportunity to receive military training in their spare time.

Air Force

- It was established in 1932. It is organised in five operational commands.

- These are Western Air Command, Southern Air Command, South-Western Air Command, Central Air Command and Eastern Air Command. In addition, Maintenance Command and Training Commands are two functional commands.

Ranks of Army, Navy and Air Force

Army

1. Field Marshal
2. General
3. Lieutenant-General
4. Major-General
5. Brigadier
6. Colonel
7. Lieutenant Colonel
8. Major
9. Captain
10. Lieutenant

Navy

1. Admiral of the Fleet
2. Admiral
3. Vice-Admiral
4. Rear-Admiral
5. Commodore
6. Captain
7. Commander
8. Lieutenant Commander
9. Lieutenant
10. Sub-Lieutenant

Air Force

1. Marshal of Indian Air Force (Honorary/war time rank)
2. Air Chief Marshal
3. Air Marshal
4. Air Vice-Marshal
5. Air Commodore
6. Group Captain
7. Wing Commander
8. Squadron Leader
9. Flight Lieutenant
10. Flying Officer

Indian Coast Guard

- Constituted as an armed force of the Indian Union on February 1, 1977, it undertakes multifarious activities like protection of sea fares, shore installations, preserving the maritime envinronment and ecology, collection of scientific data and ensuring that no poaching or smuggling takes place in India's Exclusive Economic Zone.

CIVILIAN AWARDS

Nobel Prizes

- These were instituted in 1901 by the Swedish scientist Dr. Alfred Nobel, the inventor of dynamite.
- He left a huge fortune, on the interest of which six prizes are awarded annually for Physics, Chemistry, Medicine, Peace, Literature and Economic Sciences. Indians who have received this prize so far are:
  - Dr. Rabindranath Tagore for his work Gitanjali in 1913.

- Dr. C.V. Raman for Physics in 1930
- Dr. Har Gobind Khorana,India-born US citizen, in 1968 for Medicine.
- Mother Teresa for Peace in 1979.
- S. Chandrasekhar, India-born US citizen, in 1983 for Physics.
- Amartya Sen for Economics in 1998.
- V.S. Naipaul for Literature in 2001.
- Venkatraman Ramakrishnan for Chemistry in 2009.

Kalinga Award (for the Popularization of Science)

- The award is administered by UNESCO and carries a prize of £ 1,000 sterling.
- It was started by late Biju Patnaik, the former Chief Minister of Odisha.

Ramon Magsaysay Award

- It is an annual award instituted by the Philippine Government given in the field of government service, community leadership, public service, peace and international understanding, emergent leadership, and journalism.

Pulitzer Prize

- This was founded by Joseph Pulitzer of USA. It is awarded to American men and women who have achieved distinction in literature, art, music or journalism.
- Each prize is worth $ 10,000, except for public service in which it is awarded as a gold medal.

Jawaharlal Nehru Award for International Understanding

- It is an award instituted by the Government of India in the memory of India's first Prime Minister Jawaharlal Nehru. It is open to citizens and institutions of all countries.
- The prize is of ₹ 2.5 million, convertible into foreign currency, a citation and a trophy.
- It is administered by the Indian Council of Cultural Relations.

Bharat Ratna

- This award is given for exceptional work for the advancement of art, literature and sciences and in recognition of public services of the highest order.
- Bharat Ratna is a decoration in the form of a peepal leaf, about 5.8 cm long, 4.7 cm wide and 3.1 mm thick. It is made of toned bronze. On its obverse is embossed a replica of the sun, 1.6 cm in diameter, below which the words "Bharat Ratna" in Hindi are embossed. On the reverse are the state emblem and the motto in Hindi. The emblem, the sun and the rim are made of platinum. The inscriptions are in burnished bronze.

Padma Vibhushan

- The award is given for exceptional and distinguished service in any field including service renderd by government servants.

Padma Bhushan

- The award is given for exceptional service of a high order in any field including service rendered by government servants.

Padma Shri

- The award is given for distinguished service in the field of Arts, Education, Industry, Literature, Science, Sports, Social Service, Medicine and Public Affairs. It is the fourth highest civilian award in the Republic of India.

OTHER NATIONAL AWARDS

Bharatiya Jnanpith Award

- The Jnanpith Award has been sponsored by Bharatiya Jnanpith, a cultural-literary society, founded in 1944 by the noted industrialist Shanti Prasad Jain, with the twin object of rediscovering the neglected treasure of Indian philosophy and of encouraging creative writing in various modern languages.

Rajeev Gandhi Khel Ratna Award

- This is the highest honour given for achievement in sports with a medal, a scroll of honour and cash prize of ₹ 7.5 lakh.

Arjuna Award

- It is India's highest award for excellence in sports and is given every year. It was instituted by the Government of India in 1961.
- It consists of a bronze statuette of the legendary warrior Arjuna, a scroll and a cash amount of ₹ 5 lakh.

Borlaug Award

- Instituted by Coromandel Fertilisers Ltd. of India, in the honour of the world famous wheat scientist,

Dr. Norman Borlaug, this award is given every year to an Indian scientist for outstanding contribution to agriculture and food scarcity, besides environment awareness and contribution to sustainable development.

- It carries a gold medal, a cash prize of ₹ 5 lakh and a citation.

Bhatnagar Award

- Instituted in 1957 in memory of the first Director General of CSIR, Dr. S.S. Bhatnagar, each award carries a cash prize of ₹ 5 lakh.
- This award is given for outstanding research in the field Biological Sciences, Chemical Sciences, Engineering Sciences, Mathematical Sciences, Medical Sciences and Physical Sciences.

Dada Saheb Phalke Award

- Introduced in 1969, this award is given every year for outstanding contribution to the cause of Indian cinema.
- It carries a *Swaran Kamal,* a shawl, a cash prize of ₹ 10 lakh.

Dronacharya Award

- It was instituted in 1985 to honour and convery recognition of the nation to the coaches of eminence in the country.
- It consists of a statuette of legendary archer Guru Dronacharya, a scroll and a cash prize of ₹ 5 lakh.

Gandhi Peace Prize

- The prize was instituted by the Government on October 2, 1994 on the occasion of the 125th birth anniversary of Mahatma Gandhi.

- This prize is for encouraging and promoting the significance of Gandhian values the world over.
- It carries a cash prize of ₹ 1 crore, a citation and a plaque.

Indira Gandhi Peace Prize

- It is an award instituted by the Government of India in 1986 in memory of late Prime Minister Indira Gandhi to foster creative efforts for Peace, Development and Disarmament.
- It is of the value of ₹ 25 lakh and is administered by Indira Gandhi Memorial Trust.

G.D. Birla Award for Scientific Reserach

- Instituted by K.K. Birla Foundation in 1991, the award is given in recognition of high calibre scientific resources undertaken by Indian scientists, preferably below the age of 50, who are living and working in India.
- It carries a cash prize of ₹ 1.5 lakh.

K.K. Birla Foundation Awards for Sports

- Instituted by K.K. Birla Foundation in 1991, the award is given to accord recognition to outstanding performance by sports persons.
- It carries a cash prize of ₹ 1 lakh each.

Lal Bahadur Shastri National Award

- Instituted by Lal Bahadur Shastri Institute of Management (LBSIM), the award is given to an outstanding management practitioner, educator and institution builder.
- It carries a citation, a plaque and a cash prize of ₹ 5 lakh.

Lata Mangeshker Award

- It has been instituted by the Maharashtra Government for excellence in light music. The award carries ₹ 5 lakh in cash and a citation.

Outstanding Parliamentarian Award

- It has been instituted by the Government of India for excellence in parliamentary work. It was instituted in 1992.

Rajiv Gandhi National Sadbhavana Award

- Instituted by the Indian National Congress in the memory of late Prime Minister Rajiv Gandhi. It is given on his birth anniversary which is celebrated as Sadbhavna Day (to commemorate the Golden Jubilee of Quit India Movement.)
- It carries a citation and a cash prize of ₹ 5 lakh.

Shram Awards

- These are given every year by the Government of India to workers of outstanding calibre for contribution in production and showing innovative abilities of a high order.

Tansen Samman

- It has been instituted by Madhya Pradesh Government for excellence in classical music.
- It carries ₹ 2 lakh in cash and a citation.

Vyas Samman

- It has been instituted by K.K. Birla Foundation for excellence in literature.
- It carries a cash prize of ₹ 2.50 lakh, a shawl and a citation.

IMPORTANT DATES

12th January	National Youth Day
15th January	Army Day
25th January	National Tourism Day
26th January	Republic Day
26th January	International Customs Day
30th January	Martyrs' Day
14th February	Valentine's Day
24th February	Central Excise Day
28th February	National Science Day
8th March	International Women's Day; International Literacy Day
15th March	World Consumers Rights Day
21st March	World Disabled Day; World Forestry Day
24th March	World Tuberculosis Day
26th March	Bangladesh Day
5th April	National Maritime Day
7th April	World Health Day
13th April	Jallianwala Bagh Day
18th April	World Heritage Day
22nd April	International Earth Day
1st May	Workers' Day; May Day
2nd Sunday of May	Mother's Day
3rd May	International Sun Day
8th May	World Red Cross Day
13th May	National Solidarity Day

15th May	International Day of Family
17th May	World Telecommunications Day
21st May	Anti-Terrorist Day
24th May	Commonwealth Day
31st May	World No-Tobacco Day
5th June	World Environment Day
18th June	Goa Liberation Day
26th June	International Day Against Drug Abuse and Illicit Trafficking
1st July	Doctors' Day
11th July	World Population Day
27th July	World Diabetes Day
3rd August	International Friendship Day
6th August	Hiroshima Day
9th August	Nagasaki Day
15th August	Independence Day
20th August	Sadbhavna Diwas
24th August	Sanskrit Day
29th August	National Sports Day
5th September	Teachers' Day
8th September	World Literacy Day
14th September	National Hindi Day
16th September	World Ozone Day
21st September	Engineers' Day
27th September	World Tourism Day
1st October	World Elders' Day
5th October	World Habitat Day
6th October	World Animal Day

8th October	Air Force Day
10th October	National Post Day
14th October	World Standards Day
16th October	World Food Day
24th October	UN Day
30th October	World Thrift Day
14th November	Children's Day
19th November	National Integration Day
26th November	Law Day
1st December	World AIDS Day
2nd December	World Computer Literacy Day
3rd December	International Day for Disabled Persons
4th December	Navy Day
7th December	Flag Day
10th December	Human Rights Day
23rd December	Kisan Divas/Farmers' Day

FAMOUS AIRLINES

SLA: Singapore International Airlines. It is the first airline in Asia to operate Concorde flights from London to Singapore.

Aeroflot: Russian Airlines

Cathay Pacific: Hong Kong Airlines

Garuda: Indonesian Airlines

JAL: Japan Airlines

KLM: Netherlands Airways

Lufthansa: German Airlines

PIA: Pakistan International Airlines

Quantas: Australian Airlines.

Swissair: Switzerland Airliensa

Air India: India.

WELL-KNOWN NEWS AGENCIES

- Reuters of the United Kingdom.
- Agence France Presse of France.
- United Press of America.
- International News Service of the United States.
- Tass of Russia.
- Globe (Near and Far East) News Agency
- Arab News Agency.
- NCNA (China).
- Antara of Indonesia.
- Press Trust of India
- Asian News International

Important Newspapers

Name	Place of Publication
Al Ahram	Cairo
Baltimore	Baltimore (USA)
Daily Telegraph	London
Financial Times	London
Guardian Weekly	London
New Statesman	London
The Observer	London
The Sunday Times	London
Daily Mirror	London

Daily Express	London
Dawn	Karachi
Eastern Sun	Singapore
International Herald	New York
Izvestia, Pravada	Moscow
Kabul Mail	Kabul
Le Monde	Paris
Mardeka	Jakarta
Morning Star	Canada
Pakistan Times	Lahore
People's Daily	Beijing
Red Flag	Beijing
Rude Pravo	Prague
Washington Post	Washington
Hindustan Times	Various states in India
The Times of India	Various states in India
The Tribune	Chandigarh and other states in India
The Hindu	Various states in India

FAMOUS BOOKS AND THEIR AUTHORS

Title	Author
All things Bright and Beautiful	James Herroit
An Autobiography	Jawaharlal Nehru
An Idealist View of Life	Dr. S. Radhakrishnan
Anandmath	Bankim Chandra Chartterjee

Androcles and the Lion	George Bernard Shaw
Area of Darkness	V.S. Naipaul
Arthashastra	Kautilya
Autumn Leaves	O. Pulla Reddi
Avanti Sundari	Dandi
Back To Methuselah	Geroge Bernard Shaw
Childe Harold's Pilgrimage	Lord Byron
Chinese Betrayal	B.N. Mulick
My Experiments with Truth	M.K. Gandhi
Continent of Circe	Nirad C. Chaudhuri
Coolie	Mulk Raj Anand
Curtain Raisers	K. Natwar Singh
Das Kapital	Karl Marx
David Copperfield	Charles Dickens
Death of a City	Amrita Pritam
Divine Comedy	Dante
Divine Life	Swami Shivananda
Don Juan	Lord Byron
Dream of Fair to Middling Women	Samuel Beckett
Dreams of Roses and Fire	Eyvind Johnson
Dr. Jekyll and Mr. Hyde	Robert Louis Stevenson

RECOMMENDED READING

ISBN : 9788192565583
Size : 8.5″ x 5.5″
Pages : 472
Binding : PB
Subject : Reference

Mastering English From Day One

Kavita Kumar

The book is a two-in-one monograph, a self-study and practice book for beginner to intermediate students. Each chapter is a complete unit on a specific topic in grammar and could be profitably used by learners as well as teachers. Plenty of translation exercises ensure smooth transition from native language to English.

Kavita Kumar (b. 1936) has developed an individual-based teaching approach that ensures that efficient language skills are imparted in an informal, easy manner.

ISBN : 9789382891062
Size : 7.75″ x 5.1″
Extent : 208
Binding : PB
Subject : Reference

What They Don't Teach at School

The Joy of Knowledge

Vijaya Khandurie

Do you know the name of the 13th century ruler in the Indian subcontinent who died while playing Polo?

Have you seen an animal that can clean its own ears with its tongue?

Get set for more such facts from varied fields of History, Politics, Economy, Religion, Culture, Literature, Environment, Science, Sports, Astronomy and many others, all in one book.

Vijaya Khandurie has put together interesting facts, thanks to 45 years in education.

RECOMMENDED READING

ISBN : 9788192565514
Size : 7.75" x 5.1"
Pages : 120
Binding : PB
Subject : Self-Help

Brain Building For Achievement

Herbert N. Casson

This book is a complete manual to unlock the powers of your mind and open the reservoir of your potential. Use the simple tips to build your brain strong enough to fight all odds and reach the pinnacle of success, without much ado.

Herbert N. Casson was well known as editor of London-based *Efficiency Magazine* and has to his credit a plethora of books on business efficiency, self-improvement and practical psychology.

ISBN : 9788192565507
Size : 7.75" x 5.1"
Pages : 144
Binding : PB
Subject : Self-Help

Winning Personality

The Magic Key to Success

F. Oss

Winning Personality will open gates into the unknown, hidden energies in you that you have long ignored. Oss categorises facts about personality, subconscious and conscious personal traits, and how one's personality comes into action when unlocked and maneuvered well.

"All your life you are training your mind. At home. At school. At college. In the office. When you are among friends. Whatever you do (consciously), you are using your mind, forming thought-habits, emotion-habits, and so on."